The LIFE I Led

To Marilyn
my long long longtime
friend and colleague
Love, Ralph

Ralph Graves

Also by Ralph Graves

NOVELS

Champagne Kisses, Cyanide Dreams (2001)
Orion (1993)
Share of Honor (1989)
August People (1985)
The Lost Eagles (1955)
Thanks for the Ride (1949)

NONFICTION
Objects of Desire (2003)

Outsider, Insider (1998)
With Andrew Heiskell

Martha's Vineyard: An Affectionate Memoir (1995)
With Ray Ellis

Tables of Content (1993)
With Eleanor Graves

The LIFE I Led

THE EDITOR OF AMERICA'S
MOST BELOVED MAGAZINE
TELLS HIS INSIDE, INTIMATE STORY

Ralph Graves

The magazine's first cover by Margaret Bourke-White

TIASQUAM PRESS
NEW YORK, NEW YORK

ISBN 978-1-61658-733-8

Title page illustration: Fort Peck Dam, the magazine's first cover by Margaret Bourke-White.

FIRST EDITION

Published in the United States of America by Tiasquam Press

PRINTED IN THE UNITED STATES OF AMERICA

To all my LIFE friends and colleagues
who shared those great days.

ACKNOWLEDGMENT

Way back in 1966, a young, blonde, perky girl named Bobbi Baker was hired by LIFE as a picture assistant. Because LIFE's huge picture collection was of great value and in constant demand, she was one of the few edit employees who kept her job even after the magazine folded. And today she is still there as Director of Photography for LIFE Books. She is still short, blonde and perky, and with forty-four job years behind her, she is by far the longest-term staff member in LIFE history. She has selected and controlled all the pictures for the seventy books that LIFE has published. She has also found time to marry Russell Burrows, son of the great LIFE photographer Larry Burrows.

Bobbi Baker Burrows has helped me enormously on this book. She not only supplied all the old LIFE pictures I wanted, but she researched all the names and dates I needed and sent me copies of all the articles and picture stories that I wanted to write about. I could not have written this book without her help.

All the LIFE photographs in this book are © Time Inc. and are used with permission. The photograph by Gordon Parks was shot when he worked for the Farm Security Administration. All the pictures and the photographers who took them are discussed in the book.

The LIFE I Led

INTRODUCTION

In early 1937 when I was twelve years old, I saw my first copy of a brand-new picture magazine. I thought it was wonderful. So did everybody else, millions and millions of people who saw the whole world in pictures for the first time. Year after year as I grew up, issue after issue, I still thought it was wonderful, but I never dreamed of working for it.

That magazine of course was LIFE, that famous logo, block capital white letters against a bright red field.

In 1948 when I was twenty-four years old, straight out of college, I joined the LIFE staff as a researcher. In 1969 when I was forty-four years old, I was named the top editor of LIFE. In 1972 when I was forty-eight, I had to tell my assembled staff that the magazine we all loved was dead. I still thought it was wonderful, but the advertising world had found a better, bigger, cheaper buy in television, and our readers had found that they could get the news in pictures quicker and cheaper and in moving images from that same TV source. LIFE's fabulous day, its picture window on the world, lasted thirty-six years, but it was over.

This book is not a history of LIFE nor of Time Inc., both of which have been written by others. It is neither an autobiography nor a career memoir.

This is a highly personal, highly opinionated testament to what was once the most popular, most beloved magazine in America. As the last editor of the weekly LIFE, and as the last high-ranking editor of that magazine, this is my salute.

THE JOB I DIDN'T WANT

When I was in my senior year at Harvard, I decided that after graduation I wanted to get a job in book publishing. I was an English major with very good grades, and I had been busy writing a novel. Also, I was a World War II veteran. Surely in that postwar year of 1948 some book publisher would want to hire me. Once aboard, I would be working every day with writers and editors, and I thought that would enhance my own writing career as a novelist. I now know better, but that's what I thought at the time, so I signed up with Harvard's Student Placement Center for interviews in book publishing. In those days lots of recruiters came to Harvard looking for new blood.

In due course I got a postcard from the center telling me that I had an interview in a small office in Sever Hall, 11:15 Wednesday. The card did not tell me the name of the company wanting to interview me, so as I walked to the appointment I wondered who it would be. Random House? Knopf? Maybe Little, Brown, right in Boston?

A blond, good-looking man in his thirties got up from behind the desk and walked around it to shake hands. He introduced himself as Jim Crider, waved me to a chair and took his own seat. He had a pleasant, relaxed manner.

The first thing he asked me was, "Why do you want to work for LIFE?"

My answer should have been the end of the interview. "I don't."

It took only a minute to explain that the Student Placement Center had made a mistake. I was interested in book publishing, not magazines.

Crider apologized for the inconvenience. Then he said that since he didn't have another appointment for fifteen minutes, and since I was already here, would I mind chatting? I didn't mind.

He complimented me on being an early Phi Beta Kappa and asked me what was my favorite course this year. I told him it was a small writing course with only fifteen other students and that I had just finished writing my first novel. He asked why, with my grades, I hadn't gone out for honors, and I explained that I couldn't be bothered, I was in too great a hurry to get through college and get out into the real world. Like many veterans I thought that at age twenty-four I was terribly late getting started.

At the end of our talk, Crider apologized again for the confusion and made me a most attractive offer as recompense. Next time I was in New York, he would like to buy me a nice lunch. He gave me his card.

A free and glamorous lunch in New York. I could not resist. Next time I was headed there, I called Crider. Indeed, he took me to lunch at the Gloucester House, a marvelous and expensive seafood restaurant that no longer exists. Several martinis, shad roe and old-fashioned southern biscuits, along with some very pleasant talk. At the end of the lunch, which was more perfect than I could have hoped for, Crider said why didn't I come back to the office with him and meet a few people?

I did. The talks were casual and pleasant. A week later I got a job offer. Since I hadn't heard from Random House or Knopf, I was tempted. I asked my Harvard writing professor what he thought of the idea. He puffed on his pipe, thought it over and finally said that he didn't think it would hurt my writing career as a novelist to work at LIFE for "a couple of years."

I took the job — and stayed for thirty-five years. But I am absolutely convinced that the main reason Crider and the other editors wanted to hire me was because I didn't want to work for LIFE. Back then, it was the most glamorous job in journalism, and there were very few people who said no thanks.

If you work at one place as long as I did, you are likely to hold a number of different jobs. It may be helpful to readers if I explain what mine were.

Most young men who were hired as researchers were expected to become either writers or bureau correspondents or both. As a researcher (or reporter) I worked in the Sociology Department. When given a chance to write small picture stories — textblocks, captions, headlines — I wound up writing two departments familiar to all our readers because they ran every week, Speaking of Pictures in the front of the magazine and LIFE Goes to a Party at the back. I didn't actually create these picture stories, which came from many departments and bureaus. I only wrote them.

I then was given the Nature Department, where a

researcher and I thought up our own story ideas and got a photographer assigned to shoot them. One of us would often go out with the photographer. When the pictures came in, we chose the best, made layouts with an art director, then wrote, checked and closed the story. I grew to love this department because animals always made such great pictures.

I spent two sessions in bureaus. The first was brief, only a few months in San Francisco, filling in for the regular correspondent who was ill. Later I spent two years as Chicago bureau chief, in charge of four correspondents and four photographers who covered eleven Midwestern states.

Returning to New York, I joined the Articles Department as an editor and eventually became the top editor. In 1961 I was promoted to assistant managing editor in charge of Articles, Science, Nature and Close-Ups. In 1969 I became the last managing editor of the weekly LIFE.

During and after this long LIFE career I spent a number of years in various corporate capacities. In my last five years I was Editorial Director of all Time Inc. magazines and a member of the board of directors.

None of my corporate work was half as much fun or one-quarter as exciting as LIFE.

BOURKE-WHITE AND EISENSTAEDT

By general consent, the two most famous of LIFE's great staff photographers were Margaret Bourke-White and Alfred Eisenstaedt. A half-dozen contenders could be preferred by specialists or devotees or contrarians, and I will later write about them. But the two polar stars were Bourke-White and Eisenstaedt. They happened to be among the four staff photographers listed on the masthead in the very first issue, and Bourke-White got the first cover, Fort Peck Dam, and the first lead story. Eisenstaedt got the second cover, a West Point plebe bracing at the dinner table. But the fact that they were on the staff from the very start is only incidental to their fame. Year after year, issue after issue, they kept turning out wonderful pictures. Many are classics of photojournalism.

Bourke-White: The portrait of Gandhi with his spinning wheel. The two black men deep in the diamond mines of South Africa. The Buchenwald survivors standing behind the barbed-wire fence. The relief line in Louisville, Kentucky beneath the smiling billboard boasting of "The World's Highest Standard of Living."

Eisenstaedt: The sailor kissing the nurse on V-J Day in Times Square. The exuberant children at a Paris puppet show. The strutting Michigan drum major followed by a troupe of strutting children. The glowering portrait of Nazi leader Josef Goebbels.

I worked with both of them out in the field on long photographic essays. The way a photographer handles a big assignment, the way he or she behaves under prolonged daily pressure, is both fascinating and revealing. The story that eventually runs in the magazine is the end result that everybody sees, but how those pictures got there is a different story.

PEGGY

I was still fairly new but somewhat experienced when LIFE's Sociology department decided to do a photographic essay on social classes in America. Since I was the sole researcher in the department, I would be the reporter and the photographer's assistant on the story.

The genesis was the work of a sociologist named W. Lloyd Warner. Through field work and research he had determined that American cities could be divided into six distinct social classes: upper-upper, lower-upper, upper-middle, lower-middle, upper-lower and lower-lower. This pedantic classification would never have caught LIFE's attention except for the fact that Warner had devised an arithmetic formula by which one could figure out the class that any given person belonged to. The four elements included what part of town you lived in, how you got your money (inherited was best, followed by profit from your own business, salary from a steady job, piecework), what clubs and other social organizations you belonged to.

My editor John Dille thought this would make a fine photographic essay. One of the cities Warner had studied was Rockford, Illinois. LIFE (me and a photographer) would therefore go to Rockford, pick out representatives of the six classes who were photographically interesting, make sure their credentials fitted the arithmetic formula, clear our choices with Professor Warner, and then document the six people and their homes and jobs and clubs and families in pictures and text.

The photographer selected to shoot this challenging and unusually cerebral assignment was Margaret Bourke-White.

During my brief years at the magazine I had never met her or even seen her, but there was extensive word-of-mouth. She had shot breakthrough, dramatic pictures of business and industry for *Fortune*, so when Henry Luce decided to start a new picture magazine, he picked her, a choice he never regretted. In addition to being photographically successful, she was beautiful and glamorous and daring. She wrote autobiographical books about her work, and she was a hit on the lecture circuit. During World War II as a LIFE correspondent photographer in Europe, she had triumph after triumph, getting picture stories that no other photographer could get. It was no secret that she had used her sex to the hilt — but only with generals and an occasional well-placed colonel — to go on missions that were off limits to all her competitive male photographers. At one point the widely disliked Wilson Hicks, boss of all photographers, sent a cable to Eliot Elisofon, another of LIFE's European war photographers. Hicks pointed out that Bourke-White was beating him on story after story. Why wasn't he producing better stuff? Elisofon sent back a legendary reply: "Bourke-White has a piece of equipment that I don't have."

Bourke-White had another, less-stimulating reputation. She was known for shooting picture after picture after picture on the same subject, changing cameras, changing lenses, changing exposure. Her best-known stunt in this vein was to shoot an entire roll on a U.S. route road sign. The traditional saying at LIFE was that film is cheap, meaning that it's better to overshoot than to miss a picture. Bourke-White was the exemplary of this maxim.

So, off to Rockford, Illinois with this glamorous legend on what turned out to be a month-long story.

She was in her late forties, average height, trim figure, short gray-blonde hair, a strong but lovely face, blazing eyes. Whatever she wore during our month together — skirt and jacket, a dress, a suit, or shirt and slacks, depending on that day's work program — she was always perfectly dressed, attractive but never sexually provocative. Unlike most photographers, she treated me, a young reporter, as an equal colleague. Around the office everybody called her Maggie, but she told me she preferred Peggy, so that's what I called her, then and thereafter.

In Rockford, as in most American communities, LIFE was big stuff, and the great Margaret Bourke-White was even bigger stuff. The fact that she had come to do a story on "our town" was exciting news, front page on the local newspaper. We were instantly welcome everywhere and socially sought after. *Come to cocktails. Come to lunch. Come see our country club.*

We had decided back in New York that we could not possibly reveal what we were really up to, identifying Rockford's six social classes. Nobody would cooperate with such an un-American act, and we needed full cooperation. Our declared pretense was that we wanted to record the variety of social customs and social life, and we had picked Rockford because it was such an attractive, such a very American city. While this was technically true, it was scarcely full disclosure. Everybody swallowed our bait. During the next month neither of us ever mentioned the phrase "social class."

Professor Warner had given us his map of Rockford, delineating the areas of the various social classes from top to bottom. It took Peggy and me a week to pick our six candidates and clear them with Warner. This was more an intellectual exercise than a visual one. We could pick candidates for their visual appeal, but they had to fit the arithmetic criteria. Somewhat to my surprise, Peggy was as active and interested in part two as in part one. Most photographers would not have been interested in part two but only in who would make good pictures. Peggy had a sharp mind as well as a good eye.

Now we set to work on the story. We were staying in the same hotel on the same floor, and Peggy quickly set the routine. While I ate breakfast downstairs in the coffee shop, she had a room-service breakfast. When she was dressed and ready to go to work, she phoned me to report for duty in her room.

What a mess! Pillows and wet bath towels all over the floor, robe and nightgown draped carelessly over furniture, scattered shoes and slippers, breakfast tray in sloppy disarray on the bed. Since I am compulsively neat, I was appalled. But she herself looked perfect. And her camera equipment in six large, custom-made, heavy, tan leather bags was ready to go, the bags lined up in a neat row. Okay, Ralph, pick up the bags. She didn't have to tell me. All LIFE reporters knew it was their job to lug the photographer's equipment from one place to another for as long as it took to finish the story. Yes, we had to write down captions and useful facts and quotes, but we had all been taught that if the photographer didn't get the pictures, there would be no story. So pick up the bags. So I did.

Now off to work in our rented car. Yes, the legend was true, she did shoot pictures over and over again. What the legend had not warned me about was that she was addicted to flashbulbs. Most of the stories I had worked on, the photographer used a handy 35-mm. camera and shot by natural light. Bourke-White was old-fashioned, she preferred large cameras, and she thought natural light was untrustworthy. I quickly learned to string the wires and insert the flashbulbs and then remove the bulbs after each shot and insert a new bulb. For intimate, indoor pictures Peggy would settle for a single flash with a small No. 5 bulb. But for big indoor scenes — a group picture in an auditorium — she demanded as many as six lights with the big No. 22 bulbs.

She shoots the picture, the six bulbs go off, and now I go around the auditorium changing bulbs while Peggy makes small talk with her subjects, meantime checking her cameras, perhaps changing lenses, perhaps changing cameras. Whenever she changes cameras, she wants to make sure the new one is functioning properly so, not thinking about what I'm doing in her behalf, she pushes the release button. Twice during that month a No. 22 red-hot flash goes off in the palm of my hand, leaving a burn that will last for a week. I yell in pain. Peggy realizes what she has done and calls out an abject apology, and at the end of the day she sincerely apologizes again. I accept the apology because I have come to like her, in spite of her photographic excesses.

I thought the worst excesses were two group pictures,

one of a men's singing club and one of a women's social club. None of our six social-class representatives belonged to either club, so as far as I was concerned, they were not part of our story. But Peggy insisted that they were an interesting part of Rockford social life and therefore fair game.

The men's club had a wonderful Swedish drinking song that I can still sing today because I heard it so often. At the end of the song all the men simultaneously raised their right hands high in the air. That was the picture Peggy wanted: every hand high in the air, every face looking upward into the camera. Since there are forty men in the picture, it's hard to be sure that every hand is high and that every face is looking in the right direction, so of course Peggy has to shoot it a number of times, each time with supporting flashbulbs. But she decides that they can't just raise their right hands and open their mouths, because that will not convey the true, lively spirit of their song. Therefore they must sing the whole damn song, all the way through, time after time, and when they raise their right hands at the very end on the final note, she will shoot. And then I will change the flashbulbs, and they will sing again. Peggy did not pursue the great Henri Cartier-Bresson's famous prescription that a photographer must capture "the decisive moment." She was not a decisive moment photographer.

At the end of that day when Peggy and I were eating our customary Chinese restaurant dinner, I asked her how she could ask so much of the people she was photographing. How could she expect them to put up with her endless, repetitive demands? She had obviously thought about this before, because she answered very quickly. "They see how hard I'm working to get the right picture, so they are willing to work with me."

But not always. During the picture of the women's social club, mostly older ladies, all standing together in a large space, she pulled the same stunt of shooting over and over, with time out for me to change all the flash-bulbs after every shot. Finally, as Peggy was getting set for her umpteenth shot, a large old woman in the front row said, "That's enough!" and walked off the set. I was thrilled. Peggy was astonished.

One last Rockford story. We were with our upper-upper star, a grand old lady whom both Peggy and I admired greatly. We were photographing her in her own glassed-in porch where there was plenty of natural light. But of course Peggy asked me to hold a single flash off to one side, just to make sure. Peggy shot a picture and I was changing the bulb, when the old lady suddenly leaned forward with great animation to say something, and Peggy shot the picture. I was burned again, for the third time.

I have never forgotten the expression on Peggy's face as she looked at me. So very, very sorry about the burn, really and truly sorry, Ralph, but by God she had caught that picture. The decisive moment for once. The picture ran full page in the magazine, probably the best single picture in our big twelve-page story

And when Peggy gave me a copy of her World War II book, *Purple Heart Valley,* the inscription read, "To Ralph — Who gets three purple hearts in his right hand."

A few years later Peggy contracted Parkinson's disease, ending her career. She fought it as hard as she could for as long as she could, slowly but steadily losing every battle along with every physical ability. We all knew she was dying.

On the banquet night in 1969 celebrating my appointment as managing editor, she came to the dinner in a wheelchair with her nurse. I bent down to say hello, kiss her cheek and thank her for coming. She looked at me with her still-bright eyes and tried hard to say something. I couldn't understand what she said, but I'm sure it was something very nice.

EISIE

The great Alfred Eisenstaedt was one of the first photographers I worked with as a new reporter. Since the story took place in New York City, each morning he picked me up in a taxi. I knew everybody called him Eisie, but I was brought up with good manners and was too impressed by him to do that, so I said, "Good morning, Mr. Eisenstaedt." After a few puzzled seconds he answered, "Good morning, Mr. Graves." He, too, was polite.

On the third morning when we had again exchanged this formal greeting, he came up with a solution. Look, he said, sometimes when we are working together, I will need to say something to you very quickly, maybe something important to the picture, and it takes too long to say Mr. Graves. "So to save time I will call you Rolf (his pronunciation), and you will call me Alfred."

Of course nobody, not even his wife, called him Alfred. He was always Eisie. He was a short, chunky man, physically strong and proud of it. He could do one-handed pushups, which he demonstrated frequently. He spoke good English but still with his native German accent. He was an American citizen, but because of his German background the U.S. would not let him go overseas as a war correspondent. So he missed World War II, but he shot one of its most famous pictures, the sailor kissing the nurse on V-J Day. This was only one of hundreds of "decisive moments" that Eisie shot. He was the quickest eye and hand I ever knew. When I got to know him better, he told me that sometimes when he came back from a fast-moving news story, he didn't realize until he looked at the contact sheets what he had actually shot. But whatever the picture was on whatever story, his proudest boast was that it was "needle sharp" — i.e., in perfect focus.

He had more LIFE covers than any other photographer except Philippe Halsman, who did assigned studio portraits of famous actors, actresses, TV figures, big-name politicians. Halsman did them very well, but they were all sitting ducks for possible covers. Most of Eisie's covers were pulled out of his stories by the editors because they were striking images — and always needle sharp.

Despite his age, background and experience he retained a childlike innocence — and a childlike curiosity. Everything and anything might be a picture. One of the strange relationships at Time Inc. was that Henry Luce, an intense intellectual, got along so well with Alfred Eisenstaedt, who shot the best portraits of Luce. The explanation is that they shared an overwhelming curiosity about everything.

That first story Eisie and I did together never ran in the magazine. Depending on whom you talk to, two out of three, or three out of four assigned stories never ran. In LIFE's heyday we assigned stories in the most profligate way, far more stories than could ever fit in the magazine, even when the pictures were pretty good.

When I got out of the reporter stage and became a writer and then the editor of the Nature department, Eisie and I did a big color story together on the Florida Everglades. Eisie was a cheapskate. He didn't cheat on his expense account, as a number of others did, but he took every possible advantage. On most out-of-town stories the photographer and reporter flew to the story site and rented a car, as Peggy and I had done in Rockford. However, if you used your own car on a story, LIFE allowed you seven cents a mile. Given this profit-center window, Eisie drove his new car all the way from New York to Florida, and his was the car we used, at seven cents a mile, throughout the story.

But this was a new car, and Eisie, very much in character, took pristine care of it. I don't know about today, when the Army Corps of Engineers has been destructive for years, but back in the 1950s many of the narrow little roads through the Everglades were dirt and one-track, and they threaded between trees and bushes, some of them thorny, all of them potentially scratchy to Eisie's brand-new car. He would not accept scratches, even at seven cents a mile. My most indelible memory of our weeks in the gorgeous Everglades is that I am walking down some narrow dirt road, bushes on both sides, my arms stretched out wide to indicate clearance and looking back over my shoulder toward the car, shouting to Eisie, "It's okay, keep coming."

He shot the whole story in color with a 35-mm Leica by natural light. I shudder to think of Bourke-White shooting this essay. In this wilderness where could she plug in the flashbulbs? Could she rent a portable generator? For Eisie I carried one small camera bag containing a spare Leica and different lenses and rolls of film. In the process of doing the story, we both learned the difference between an anhinga and a cormorant and a heron, and we did a lot of alligator pictures, and we knew we had to find a roseate spoonbill, as indeed we did.

We also got chiggers, those tiny, nasty red bugs that itch like crazy, worse than poison ivy. My case was far worse than Eisie's. I think he was just a little bit jealous. Why was I, a young editor, suffering worse than he was?

All through the Everglades story we had dinner together every night, just as Peggy and I had done in Rockford. Peggy had been a fascinating dinner companion, talking about many dramatic events in her life but equally curious about my own past. Eisie was much less interesting, although his past was almost as colorful as hers.

What I best remember about Eisie's and my dinners was key lime pie. We both loved it and ordered it every single night in every restaurant. When the dessert plates were set down in front of us, Eisie carefully dipped his little finger in the whipped cream, then rubbed it against his thumb.

He looked at me and announced his verdict: "Greasy. It's fake." He pronounced it "Greezy." He taught me that real whipped cream always feels smooth to the touch but fake whipped cream out of a can or bottle is always greasy.

In spite of all the fake whipped cream our Everglades essay ran for many pages, a true success.

Eisie and I had both been going to Martha's Vineyard for summer vacations for many years. He was annoyed that I had been going two years longer than he. One cold gray December day in the office, one of us said, "I wonder what it's like now at the Vineyard." Neither of us could later remember who said it, but we both knew at once that it was a story: What happens to a popular summer resort in winter?

We whizzed through a long photo essay in two weeks. Partly because we both knew the territory. We didn't have to ask directions to Chilmark or Oak Bluffs, we knew where the town meetings were held, and we knew the people to ask for help. But mostly because Eisie was so quick. He sized up every situation and every person, took his pictures and moved on to the next.

My favorite picture in the story was a violation of LIFE rules. We staff members were all taught that we must never appear in a picture. *Stay out of the picture because if you're in it we won't run it.* On one cold blustery day Eisie wanted to take a picture of a deserted beach that, in sunlit summer, would have been jammed with swimmers and sunbathers. For scale and human interest, he wanted a solitary figure in his picture, and on this awful day with winter waves crashing on the shore, there was nobody in sight. I volunteered to serve. I walked down the beach, hunched against the cold and careful to keep my face turned away from the camera. Great picture! It ran in the magazine across a full spread. And I got to write the caption for my own picture, something about "a lonely islander."

Eisie had a few special interests, but all he really wanted to do was take pictures. Take pictures and see them published, first in the magazine and then in a series of books. When he went on vacation to the Vineyard, he always took a camera on his daily walks and drives. Whenever we ran into each other at the Vineyard, he took pictures of me and my family, mostly for friendship, but partly just to be taking pictures. They are, of course, the best family pictures we have.

He could not stand idleness. On one occasion at LIFE a top editor congratulated him on a set of his pictures he had just taken. Eisie didn't even say thank you. What he said was, "I have been in the office for four days, and I don't have an assignment."

Unlike Peggy, Eisie lived a long time in excellent health and kept taking pictures.

He was world famous. He won many awards and tributes and medals, and book after book emerged from his vast collection. He spent day after day in his office, going over all his pictures, making sure they were in perfect order and fully documented. He was leaving his collection to LIFE, but he didn't trust us to organize it.

In his nineties he unraveled. He wound up in a wheelchair, unable to do anything for himself. Worst of all, unable to take pictures.

I had lunch with him at the Vineyard three days before he died. He was profoundly depressed. He could still talk clearly, but that was all. The man who used to do one-handed pushups could not now do anything for himself.

It was very sad, so I tried to cheer him up. I said, "Eisie, remember that you are famous. You are the most famous photographer in the world. Everybody knows your name, everybody knows your pictures, everybody respects you."

For a lovely moment his face brightened. Big smile. "You would not believe how many letters I get! Letters from everywhere!"

Yes, Eisie, I believe it. I think he was the best photojournalist ever.

MY WHITE WEASEL

LIFE researchers had many little chores. We went out on stories with photographers, carried their equipment, took captions and then typed up our information so that the writer could write the story that would appear in the magazine. Also, after the writer had done his deed, the researcher had the responsibility of checking the story to make sure that every word, every name, every number was accurate.

This last was not a popular role, neither with the researcher who had to perform it nor with the writer nor his editor who had to endure the result. The magazine loved superlative statements: "the best," "the most," "the longest," "the fastest," so that is what the writer wrote and that is what his editor approved. Then along came the nasty, tiresome researcher who, after checking various sources, announced that no, it was not the longest, it was only the fourth longest. The writer then had to supply a weasel, a corrective phrase that converted an unacceptable inaccuracy into an acceptable fact. The commonest, easiest weasel was "one of," as in "one of the longest." But there were many others, such as "some" or "among" or if the so-called fact was actually in dispute, "according to certain authorities." Nobody liked weasels. They weakened sentences and took up precious space. But if a researcher failed to catch an inaccuracy, and if a reader or in-house watchdog caught the mistake, the researcher got a dreaded Errors Report, with many carbon copies sent to various authorities.

I hated checking and wasn't very good at it, but I did have one special achievement.

I inherited a story from a researcher who had moved to a different department. She had supervised the photographs and a technical drawing, and she had product information handouts from the manufacturer, but she had not had time to do the necessary research for the writer. I had not had time to do it either, but I was suddenly told that the story was closing, so I better get cracking.

The story was about a new mechanical device called a heat pump. It was designed to create heat through electrical energy at a lower cost than other sources of heat. The whole point of our story was that it might save people money on their heating bills. But the more I talked to experts, the less likely this seemed. It became clear that the heat pump was strictly an experiment. It was not the wave of the future and might never be.

I told my writer and my division editor that I thought we should drop the story. Nonsense! Departments were in fierce competition for space in the magazine, the heat pump was scheduled to close, and we would proceed to close it. The writer and I would have to work it out together.

My biggest challenge came from an electrical engineer who patiently explained to me that electrical energy was far too expensive for the heat pump to be practical. It would be economical only in a place where electricity was dirt cheap. "Like where?" I asked. "Like TVA," he said, "the Tennessee Valley Authority where they give it away for nothing."

The writer and I did work it out, but twice we had to appeal to our division editor to resolve a dispute. In the middle of the opening textblock, to the best of my memory, this negotiated sentence appears: "Some tests indicate that the heat pump may prove to be more economical than other systems in some areas." If you read this quickly, it sounds as though the heat pump might save you money. But here is the translation: "Some tests (*not all tests*) indicate (*only indicate, nothing more*) that the heat pump may prove (*not prove*) to be more economical than other systems (*other not specified*) in some areas (*if you live in the TVA area*).

Because I had managed to get five weasels into a single published sentence, the division editor awarded me The Order of the White Weasel.

LUCE

I have read two books about Henry Luce that did not do him justice. I skipped others that sounded equally unimpressive. Some day there will be a good one. Meantime, here are a few personal stories about a man I admired and liked, even though I often disagreed with his rigid editorial positions.

I was lucky. Thanks to his quirky work habits, I spent a lot of time with him, one-on-one, when I was still only a thirty-five-year-old articles editor. Luce had founded Time Inc., he ran it and all its magazines. He basically owned it. Although he had titles, we all referred to him as The Proprietor.

The Proprietor dealt mostly with his half-dozen managing editors and the dozen or so assistant managing editors. Many lofty discussions about national and international policy and how his magazines should treat them. He held weekly lunches with these editorial powerhouses at which he usually ignored his food and asked a series of penetrating questions. Sometimes he delivered long monologues about some subject that was on his mind or some book he had just read or some prominent person he had just met. Many editors preferred the monologues. Although they were boring, at least they were not threatening, like his questions.

But once in a while Luce would think of a problem on one of his magazines that needed fixing. He would then explore the problem in depth, harass the appropriate editors, reach a conclusion and decree a solution. He would then stick that solved problem in a mental pigeonhole where he need not think of it again. That's done, now then, on to the next problem —

Luckily for me, he decided that the major weekly LIFE article needed to be defined. He had no particular complaint about individual articles, or even about the articles in general, but the subjects were scattered all over the place. The reader, including The Proprietor himself, never knew from one week to the next what to expect. Luce decided that the LIFE article needed to be clearly and precisely defined. The reader should know, when he picked up each week's magazine, that the article would fit into a certain pattern. This meant that Luce must have extended talks with the articles editor, interrogate him, challenge him, persuade him and eventually herd him into some suitable corral.

The man who warned me about this approaching ordeal was Luce's senior editorial assistant, Bill Furth. A former *Fortune* editor, he was an amiable, avuncular older man, a bit overweight. Like many of us, including me but not Luce, he was a hearty drinker but, perhaps because of age, it showed more on him, a flushed complexion, a slight tendency to nod off. He was a perfect counterpart to his boss, nonthreatening, easy to like and talk to. The oddest facet of his job was to hold himself in readiness the day of Luce's weekly lunch with his top editors. If the acceptance list came to what Luce considered the unlucky total of thirteen, Bill Furth was, at the last minute, ordered to attend. If the total was any other number, Furth was free to lunch on his own. Once he was sprung, it would be hard for him to make a last-minute lunch date. I wondered if Bill, in his slightly insulting standby role, held some inferior employee in a similar standby role to join him at lunch.

Furth came to my office to give me the news. This was unusual. Most exalted people, both in edit and publishing, summoned people to their office. It was part of their loftiness. The sole exception I remember is Andrew Heiskell, LIFE publisher and then chairman for twenty years, who liked to roam the halls, dropping in on people he wanted to talk to. Furth told me that I would be getting a call from Luce to discuss the LIFE articles. Perhaps it would be a good idea for me to look back over the articles of the last couple of years, just to refresh my memory and be ready to discuss them. Maybe to defend them. Luce had read almost all of them, Bill said, except those that dealt with some form of physical pain. Like, for instance, the long article we had recently run on the Coconut Grove fire where hundreds had burned or suffocated. "Harry," said Bill as a tip, "doesn't like that kind of story. I suggest you don't bring it up."

Harry.

Everybody called him one of two things. To the huge bulk of us, if we ever spoke to him at all, he was Mr. Luce. High-level insiders called him Harry, but only after making dead certain in their own minds that this would be permissible. Nobody ever called him Henry — except for one person, President Dwight Eisenhower. Luce, both by personal effort and in the pages of his magazines, had vigorously supported the nomination of Eisenhower over

Senator Robert Taft, and then (of course) supported Eisenhower for the presidency against Democrat Adlai Stevenson. Luce and Eisenhower had met, but they did not know each other. Luce was a powerful voice in the Republican Party, and when Eisenhower won the election, he wrote Luce a grateful letter that began "Dear Henry." I cannot personally vouch for this, but I was told Luce remarked, "I helped make him President, he ought to know enough to write, 'Dear Harry.'"

At the time of the approaching investigation, I still called him Mr. Luce. I had been an editor in the Articles Department for five years and the boss for the last two. It was the best job I had in my thirty-five years in the company. Not the highest ranking, but the one I liked best. I reviewed our articles during that whole period. Of course there were some dogs, but not too many. My review confirmed what I already thought and had practiced from the start. The main LIFE article could be about *any* interesting subject or person or story. The entire world was the subject. The very last thing it needed was a restrictive definition.

Our duel began when Luce and I met for dinner at Manhattan's prestigious Lotos Club. He brought Bill Furth along, I don't know why, since Bill played no part in the discussion. Perhaps Bill provided some form of personal protection. Luce was not comfortable with new people. A table for three, Luce and I across from each other, Bill Furth in between. Luce was then in his early sixties, medium-tall, trim, wearing heavy, dark-rimmed glasses under the very bushiest gray eyebrows.

I have mentioned that my talks with Luce were one-on-one, and indeed they were, even though a third person was present. Luce and I argued and arm wrestled through three long, long dinners, Bill Furth nodding off while Harry (so addressed by me at the second dinner) and I debated. It was good fun for us both. Every time he proposed a limitation on what the LIFE article should be, I was able to mention articles we both admired that did not fit into his restriction. "Well," he would say, "all right, we have to broaden that a little bit." Then he would come back with some other restriction or suggestion, always provocative, always stimulating, which I would try to counter with other good articles that shouldn't be ruled out.

While I was able to fight off any severe definition, we were able to agree, very congenially, that certain *kinds* of articles were indeed preferable. Important national or international issues. Profiles of important people. Articles by significant writers. Strong narrative human stories. But also, with Harry's grudging agreement, anything really special that we cannot predict or define in advance.

This settlement was, for me, the equivalent of the seventeenth-century writer Henry Aldrich who came up with this prescription:

> If all be true that I do think,
> There are five reasons we should drink:
> Good wine — a friend — or being dry —
> Or lest we should be by and by —
> Or any other reason why.

The principal result of these meetings was not the definition or nondefinition of the LIFE article, but that Harry

Luce and I got to know each other and had a lively time arguing together. From then on we got along very well.

Many years later when I retired and sent my papers to Archives, a friend in that department sent me a one-page memo from Bill Furth to Luce that she thought I might enjoy seeing. Indeed I did. The memo informed Luce that there was this young articles editor that he should be aware of. It described some good qualities that I was said to possess, and it pointed out that I had recently been offered the top editing job at a major book publisher, but had turned it down to stay at LIFE. *Keep an eye on him.*

Of course I could not help wondering if this memo had been the real reason for Luce's sudden interest, those many long years ago, in defining the LIFE article. By the time I saw Bill's memo, Luce and Furth were both dead, so there was nobody I could ask. Very flattering, if true, that Luce was just trying to check me out and see if the memo was true. But I decided this could not be. Luce couldn't have been so good an actor. Those dinner arguments were genuine. He had really wanted to pin down the LIFE article. The fact that in the process he learned something about me, and I about him, was a bonus.

Luce was noted for his last-minute invitations to lunch. I don't know if he realized how discourteous he was. I suppose if you're The Proprietor, it doesn't matter. All of us who were high enough in rank to get such an invitation knew exactly what to answer. After his secretary called, Luce would get on the phone in person: "You free for lunch?" Whatever you might have scheduled, the only possible answer was an enthusiastic "Yes, sir."

But on one occasion, receiving that abrupt phone call, I took my career in my hands. I said, "Harry, I'm sorry but I can't."

For the last several years a small group of LIFE editors and writers had been lunchtime regulars at a Chinese restaurant called Canton Village. In return for our year-long patronage, the hostess, Pearl Wong, rewarded six of us with a Chinese New Year's banquet. We paid for the lunch, but the drinks — multiple martinis followed by stingers — were on the house. Since I was the most regular of the regulars, Pearl asked me to pick the attendees, any six.

So I apologized to Luce. "Today I'm the host of a Chinese New Year's lunch."

Since Luce had been born in China and was a passionate patriot, I thought I stood a fighting chance to be forgiven. I got more than that.

"Who's coming?" Luce asked.

I told him the other five guests. He knew four of them but about the fifth he asked, "Who's that?"

I identified him as a staff writer and former Mid-East bureau chief.

Satisfied that these were solid citizens, Luce asked, "Can I come?"

Only one conceivable answer to that. "Yes, of course."

As soon as we hung up, I called the other five men and told them the bad news. It would obviously be a very different New Year's lunch. No fun-loving orgy this time, but at least it might be interesting. Then I called Pearl.

"Mr. Luce? *The* Mr. Luce?"

So everybody, especially Pearl herself, was nervous as we sat down to a round table for seven. Everybody except Luce, who was uncharacteristically delightful. I would never again see him so relaxed and so entertaining. Two of my friends had never before had a meal with Luce and didn't realize how extraordinary this occasion was.

We all ordered our martinis, Luce ordered some milder drink, and then he began to talk about China. For a welcome change he wasn't talking about the excellence of Chiang Kai-Shek or the wickedness of the Communists but about his own boyhood as the son of Presbyterian missionaries, good anecdotes, good yarns. This was not one of his boring monologues. He was telling stories, we all felt free to ask questions and make comments, and these would set him off on new stories. He was laughing with us.

None of us wanted to risk The Proprietor's disapproval by calling for another martini. Instead, we held our empty glasses behind our chair seats, a waiter picked them up and a fresh drink would soon silently arrive. I don't think Harry noticed, but I don't think he would have cared. He was having too good a time.

Now here came Pearl with the very first dish of the banquet, a large platter with a bright metal cover to keep the contents piping hot. She held the platter in front of Luce and removed the cover. It was the Canton Village's special *dim sum,* a dish Pearl knew we all liked.

Luce looked at it. "Ha!" he said. "Just what I like. Real peasant food!"

The word "inscrutable" is frequently applied to the Chinese, but Pearl's face was definitely scrutable. In all the later years when she ran her own famous restaurant under her own name, I doubt that anybody ever again accused her of serving peasant food.

Except for Pearl's wounded feelings, the lunch was a grand success. Luce ate everything, obviously enjoying himself the whole way. At last he looked at his watch, said he had to get back for a meeting, and thanked us for inviting him. He stood up, gave us a little wave and walked out.

The six of us knew we had shared a unique Chinese New Year's. We celebrated with stingers on the rocks.

If I had to pick one dominant characteristic for Luce it would be curiosity. Anything new, anything he didn't know about, ignited his interest. Here is one small example. In 1963 when I was assistant managing editor of LIFE and running the magazine during the managing editor's absence, I attended one of Luce's weekly lunches for his top editors. After random talk of this and that, Luce swung around on me and asked, "What's LIFE's lead story this week?"

That was an easy question because we had been planning it and working on it for some time. "It's The Beatles."

The big bushy eyebrows shot up. "What's that?"

This lunch was before the Ed Sullivan TV show that introduced The Beatles to America, so Luce could perhaps be excused for his question. I don't think he had any interest in popular music anyway, but by this time many of us had already heard "I Want to Hold Your Hand" and "She Loves You."

I explained that The Beatles were a hit English music group — but a lot more besides.

Luce spent the rest of that lunch finding out from me everything about The Beatles. How many were there? What were their names? Why are they so popular? How would you describe their music? What do you mean, long hair? How long? Why is that important? Why do their clothes matter? What kind of clothes? Drugs? — what kind of drugs? Liverpool? *Liverpool*?

Because I was myself an ardent Beatles fan and had prepared our lead story, I was able to answer almost all his questions. A few other editors chimed in with additional details. The best outside contribution, reported by me, came from my own boss George Hunt. He had been driving his teenage daughters somewhere, the radio was playing "I Want to Hold Your Hand," nearing the end of that song, and they were approaching an underpass. His daughters screamed at him to slow down, slow down, don't reach the underpass, because they wanted to hear that wonderful final chord.

Luce left that lunch armed to the teeth to tell the world about The Beatles. As I am sure he did.

Luce retired in 1964 when he was sixty-six. He appointed Hedley Donovan, the managing editor of *Fortune*, to take his place as editor-in-chief. (More about Donovan in a later chapter.)

When Luce died three years later on February 28, 1967, Donovan was out of the country on a business trip and so was my Managing Editor George Hunt. I was in charge of LIFE, and I decided instantly that I would put

Luce on our cover. Alfred Eisenstaedt had shot some excellent, fairly recent portraits of Luce. I got them up from the Picture Collection and picked one.

Not so fast.

Tom Griffith was sitting in for Hedley Donovan as editor-in-chief, just as I was sitting in for George Hunt. Griffith said no, Luce should not be on LIFE's cover. If anywhere, Luce should be on the cover of *Time*, the magazine that founded the company.

I was furious. I didn't care what *Time* did or didn't do, I wanted Luce on LIFE's cover.

Griffith still said no. I sent Eisie's picture to be engraved, just so we could still use it if minds could be changed. Then I called George Hunt (in Australia, I think), explained my problem and then got Tom Griffith on the same phone. The argument grew so fierce between them that I said I was going to hang up, and I did.

Griffith's answer remained no for LIFE. And I learned that *Time* wasn't going to put Luce on the cover either — it would look too self-serving, and besides, *Time* doesn't put dead people on the cover.

I got a call from my friend Osborn Elliott, the editor of *Newsweek* and a former *Time* editor. Oz was only calling to express his sympathy, but then we got to talking about covers. I told Oz about my war with Griffith about LIFE's cover and then about the fact that *Time* didn't plan to do a cover either.

"Good God!" Oz said. "Then I'll do it on *Newsweek*. Have you got a good picture I could use?"

I sure did. I sent Oz an excellent but different picture from Eisie's set of Luce portraits, and that is what *Newsweek* ran.

Hank Luce, Harry's son, and I both think we were personally responsible for finally persuading *Time* to put Luce on its cover that week. Hank thought he had talked Griffith and *Time*'s managing editor into doing it. I thought that *Newsweek*'s cover use of Eisie's portrait had at last driven *Time* to come to its reluctant senses. Whatever the genesis, *Time* could not run another photographic portrait, since *Newsweek* already had the fine Eisie picture I had given them. And now it was much, much too late for *Time* to create one of its traditional, classy art portraits. So it created a flimsy last-minute, half-ass sketch portrait.

At LIFE I was still forbidden to run a Luce cover — that was now *Time*'s reluctant privilege. So I wound up running a nothing cover of a Vietnam parachute jump, with the main cover billing on Luce. At least I did run a long commemorative lead story on The Proprietor.

I still wonder today what Harry would have thought about these ridiculous shenanigans. Here were his two most important magazines niggling and jockeying over his death. Would he have been appalled, as I was? Or might he have shrugged and been amused?

I didn't know him well enough to answer that. He was a complicated man.

THE REAL HOAX

Unless you are Franklin Roosevelt or Winston Churchill, the chances of seeing yourself portrayed in a Hollywood movie under your own name are very slim. But that happened to me in the Richard Gere movie *The Hoax*, about Clifford Irving's famous phony autobiography of Howard Hughes. Because LIFE bought the magazine rights to Irving's fraud from the book publisher McGraw-Hill, and because I was LIFE's top editor, a character named Ralph Graves appeared in the movie.

The actor who portrayed me was short, bald and looked mildly effeminate. Since I am none of these, I took a good deal of kidding from friends and family who saw the movie. However, what most offended me about the Ralph Graves character was not his appearance but the fact that he had so little to do with the movie's story. After all, I was a central figure in this caper. Several friends and colleagues have suggested that I write a whole book about it. I was the one who, under a severe pledge of total secrecy, actually bought the magazine rights for LIFE. From that day through all the investigating and challenging and unraveling, right up to the final denouement, I was an active participant in everything that happened. I spent substantial time with Clifford Irving himself, some of it at crucial moments.

I was also the biggest single fool in the shipload of fools at McGraw-Hill and Time Inc.

I first heard of Clifford Irving from Beverly Loo, the short, sharp, round-faced Chinese-American woman who handled all magazine and newspaper rights for the giant book publisher McGraw-Hill. In the past I had bought several book excerpts from Beverly for LIFE. The way this works, the publisher thinks it has a forthcoming book that would be a good bet for excerpting by a magazine, the bigger the magazine the better. If the magazine agrees, it buys the rights to a prepublication excerpt. This is good publicity for the book, it's extra money for the publisher and the author, and it's good content for the magazine. Everybody wins. Beverly Loo and I had made several of these deals to the mutual benefit of LIFE and McGraw-Hill, but nothing of this magnitude.

Like most book-magazine deals, and like most deals in the entire spectrum of publishing, this one took place not in the office but in a restaurant over drinks and lunch. I had to lean across the table to hear Beverly, who kept her voice low to preserve secrecy.

McGraw-Hill had this author Clifford Irving. He had been no big deal until now. They had published a couple of his books, no big successes, although one of them about the art forger Elmyr de Hory, had done pretty well. This book (appropriately titled *Fake!*) was a major factor in what she was about to tell me. But before she told me, she wanted my promise that I would tell no more than two people in all of Time Inc. She said she knew that what she was about to propose was too important and too expensive for me to agree to all by myself, even though I was the managing editor of LIFE. McGraw-Hill had chosen to approach me because LIFE had huge circulation and would pay top dollar, and because Beverly had guaranteed her bosses that I could be trusted with their tremendous secret.

Pretty exciting! Already half hooked, I gave her my promise.

Years ago Howard Hughes, the multifascinating, multireclusive multibillionaire, had disappeared into oblivion. He talked to nobody. He was invisible to the world. Holed up on the entire top floor of a hotel in the Bahamas, fiercely protected by trusted aides and bodyguards, he had not been seen or interviewed for years. Every journalist on every publication would have given anything for an interview or even just a photograph. All of us would have given anything to get to Hughes. None of us did.

But, said Beverly Loo, Howard Hughes had read Clifford Irving's book about Elmyr de Hory and had decided that this was the perfect writer to tell his own story, which he had decided he was now at last ready to tell. Irving had received handwritten letters from Howard Hughes proposing this project and spelling out details, including the price and a demand that total secrecy be maintained until the book was finished. Hughes, famously undependable and erratic, reserved the right to change his mind if he was not completely satisfied.

"Okay," I said. "We're interested. Show me the Howard Hughes letters, and show me this Clifford Irving. I won't believe it till I see it. But yes, we are definitely, seriously interested."

Looking back from a distance of forty years, I can

now see that this proposal was absolute bullshit. I don't blame Beverly Loo or McGraw-Hill — or at least not terribly much. They were true believers because they could see a huge publishing bonanza. Besides, they were not in the journalism business, which is very different from the publishing business.

But I was in the journalism business. I should have asked McGraw-Hill and asked myself a flock of tough questions. Why would Howard Hughes have read such an obscure book by such an obscure author? Why would he even have heard of the book? And even in the unlikely event that Hughes did read it, why would he have been impressed? Why would he have had the slightest interest in an art forger? And why would Howard Hughes, invisible for years, decide that he now wanted to tell his story — and tell it to, of all people, this minor figure Clifford Irving?

Answer: journalists are suckers for a scoop. And Howard Hughes was at that time perhaps the most super-scoop in the world. As Coleridge put it long long ago, "willing suspension of disbelief." We all wanted to believe this was true, me most of all — and with the least justification. I should have known better. I had not only been a professional journalist for thirty years, but I worked for a company that made a fetish of checking everything for accuracy before publication. Ah yes, but so what? Hughes's reputation for secrecy and weird behavior enhanced the possibility that this nonsense might actually be true.

I duly told this great, wonderful secret to my allotted two people: Hedley Donovan, Time Inc.'s editor-in-chief, and David Maness, who had worked with me for years on

LIFE articles. Neither had ever heard of Clifford Irving, but both were intrigued and waited to hear more.

Donovan said much later, after the hoax had unraveled, that if he had only read Clifford Irving's art forgery book way back then, he would have smelled the rat. The book just wasn't good enough to have captured Hughes's admiration. Maybe so, but that was Monday morning quarterbacking. I, however, did take the trouble to read Irving's book way back then and found it interesting if not compelling. How does an art forger get away with creating so many Matisse and Picasso drawings and selling them right and left? How does he convince art collectors and art dealers and art experts that these forgeries are the real thing? Besides, who knew how the devious mind of Howard Hughes worked? Maybe he just ate this stuff up. Anyway that is what I eagerly chose to believe.

As for my other confidant, David Maness, he and I had been working together on another top-top-secret project, the clandestinely taped memoirs of Nikita Khrushchev. All during the endless months of preparation we had called it "the Jones Project." The tapes were smuggled out of Russia, translated and published in LIFE to great acclaim in late 1970 under the title *Khrushchev Remembers*. Maness and I trusted each other to hold a big secret close to our chests for a long time. It had worked on Khrushchev, why not on Hughes? However, to Dave's credit, he never trusted Clifford Irving the way he trusted Nikita Khrushchev. He never liked Irving.

The person I should have told, if I had known enough to do so, was a *Time* correspondent and former Los Angeles bureau chief named Frank McCulloch. He actually knew Howard Hughes, knew him quite well, in the days before his disappearance. He had talked to Hughes many times over the years and in fact had the last long interview with Hughes before he vanished. If I had talked to him, he would have raised many legitimate doubts and asked many sharp questions. Perhaps if he had had a crack at Clifford Irving at the very beginning, he could have stopped him cold. On the other hand, perhaps not. When McCulloch was finally brought into the act, suspicions were already high. After talking to Irving and reading the Hughes manuscript, McCulloch switched back and forth between belief and disbelief.

In April 1971, I first met Clifford Irving. Shepherded by Beverly Loo, we had lunch together at Barbetta's, a restaurant in the West Forties with mediocre food but good drinks and a very quiet atmosphere, a perfect spot to hatch a plot.

We will start the account of this lunch with Irving's description of me in his book, because it is such an improvement over the movie's depiction of me. "I liked Ralph immediately: a man in his late forties, with a deep voice and blue eyes whose keenness was curiously softened by his glasses."

Now for Irving. He was tall, a couple of inches over six feet, and looked athletic. A full head of neat brown hair. He had a lean, attractive face, a strong nose and a healthy tanned complexion, no doubt the result of outdoor life on his sunny Spanish island home of Ibiza. His conversation was lively and intelligent. He had a quick sense of humor and an easy, sleazy charm. I enjoyed his company, then and later.

Under prodding from Beverly, he told anecdotes about

his secret meetings with Howard Hughes. These were interesting, to be sure, but what I wanted was to see his handwritten letters from Hughes. LIFE had recently published a two-page reproduction of a long handwritten letter from Hughes to his lawyer, Chester Davis. In anticipation of this lunch with Irving I had looked at it carefully this morning. Hughes had written on lined yellow paper. I visually memorized the style of his handwriting.

At lunch Irving brought out a photocopy of his handwritten letter from Howard Hughes, explaining that the original, written on lined yellow paper, was safely locked away. I am not, of course, a professional handwriting analyst, but the writing looked absolutely the same as the pages I had just studied in LIFE. I said so.

Irving, who of course was not a professional forger, smiled. With relief? With pleasure? He had used the LIFE reproduction to perfect his Hughes forgeries. And that was not the last help he would get from LIFE.

This story is full of irony, as well as chicanery.

I signed a contract with McGraw-Hill that would permit us to publish three long excerpts from the finished book. The price was a then-whopping $250,000. However, we were protected by an escape clause in the contract. If the notoriously unpredictable Hughes failed to approve the Irving manuscript, LIFE would be released from the contract and would not owe McGraw-Hill a penny. In the end, of course, we did not owe McGraw-Hill any part of the $250,000, but my guess is that we spent that much money tracking down the hoax.

Clifford Irving went off to work on his book with his friend-colleague-researcher, Richard Suskind. All the material that supposedly was coming straight from the mouth of Howard Hughes in a series of clandestine meetings in Mexico and the Caribbean was actually coming from many different documents including, alas, vital details from the Time Inc. files. Irving didn't steal them. I gave them to him.

Cliff (we are now on friendly first-name terms) said that it might be very helpful to him if he could get a look at our company files on Hughes. They might help him to ask Howard sharper questions. Since we were now on the same team and eager to get the best possible book, I said sure, why not, but he could not take the files out of the Time-Life Building. He would have to read them right there, and he could not take them away.

No problem for Cliff. Dave Maness put the big bushel of files in their well-organized, well-labeled manila envelopes in a small office and locked Cliff inside. The files proved an invaluable bonanza. Cliff photographed many, many pages with a handheld camera. One of the documents he photographed was Frank McCulloch's last long interview with Hughes, never published by *Time*. (Bear this in mind when we reach the last quarter of this game.)

The rough manuscript that Cliff eventually produced was almost a thousand pages long in question-and-answer form. Working from all the documents they had collected, both published and unpublished, he and his partner Suskind had taken turns pretending to be Hughes while the other asked brief questions. They had taped and then transcribed these "interviews." While they invented many lively little touches, the huge bulk was based on careful research. Make no mistake, they did an enormous amount of hard work.

The reading took place over two days, September 13 and 14, 1971. There were three McGraw-Hill readers, including Albert Leventhal, the head of the company's trade book division. There were two LIFE readers, Dave Maness and me. The reading took place in Cliff's two-room suite at the Elysee Hotel on East 54th Street. Maness, who had been a *Collier's* editor before he came to LIFE, told me that the Elysee had been a great favorite of the nearby *Collier's* staff because it was a handy and totally accessible spot for illicit assignations. In fact, said Dave, we all called it the "Easy Lay."

We read the long manuscript, page by page, passing the pages down the line from one to another. Both Dave and I thought it was a knockout for LIFE. There were many truly tiresome passages, especially about arcane aeronautic detail. But the beauty of excerpting a book for magazine publication is that you can take all the good stuff and ignore all the boring stuff, of which there was a large amount. We could leave that problem for Albert Leventhal and his editors to solve for their book. LIFE would just pick out the gold and run.

Everybody was confident. The large McGraw-Hill checks to Hughes had been deposited in a Credit Suisse bank account in Zurich, and the canceled checks endorsed by "H.R. Hughes" had come back to McGraw-Hill. We were all in clover.

McGraw-Hill announced the forthcoming book on December 7, Pearl Harbor Day. (I promised you irony.) Dell bought the paperback rights for a fortune, and Book-of-the-Month Club bought the book-club rights for a fortune. The money was rolling in.

But Hughes's lawyer Chester Davis instantly denounced the book as a fraud. This did not bother either LIFE or McGraw-Hill. Davis, by his own admission, had never even met his client, and the denouncement had come from Davis, not from Hughes himself. We waited for Howard to tell Davis to knock it off. We waited in vain.

One week after the Pearl Harbor Day announcement, Frank McCulloch, now New York bureau chief for the Time-Life News Service, got a call from an old Hughes associate. The associate told Frank that Hughes wanted to talk to him. The phone call had to be placed by Chester Davis and could not be taped.

The event took place on the corporate 34th floor of the Time-Life Building. In one office were McCulloch, Time Inc. Lawyer Jack Dowd, Time Inc. vice-president and spokesman Donald Wilson, along with Chester Davis and his supporting lawyers who would later be able to corroborate whatever happened. In a separate office down the hall were Cliff, his colleague Richard Suskind, a small McGraw-Hill contingent and me. None of us could hear the phone conversation. We were all standing by, waiting to be told the result.

It was the only time in this long caper that I saw Clifford Irving lose his cool. He fidgeted, he doodled, he complained, he told us it could not possibly be the real Hughes, it could only be an imposter, a fraud, a fake. Finally he could not stand the suspense. He announced that he and Suskind had a dinner date at a restaurant with a lawyer friend, and by God they were leaving. And by God they left.

Frank McCulloch was having a half-hour phone conversation with a voice that he believed, in his best judgment, was that of Howard Hughes himself. Hughes denied that he had ever met Clifford Irving or worked on a book. He threatened a lawsuit.

You would think that would be the end of it right there. Surely reasonable men would now come to their senses and realize that the jig was up. But not so fast.

Once the Hughes book had been announced publicly, McGraw-Hill and LIFE decided to buttress their case against any possible challenge, legal, competitive or otherwise. We collected every scrap of authentic, officially accepted Hughes handwriting, along with the Hughes handwritten letters to Irving and the canceled McGraw-Hill checks endorsed by "H.R. Hughes" for deposit in the Swiss bank. We gave this entire package to the eminent handwriting analysis firm of Osborn Associates. They were top of the line in the field of disputed documents. Their testimony was accepted in court cases.

The main meetings between McGraw-Hill top brass and Time Inc. top brass, including lawyers for both sides, took place in the McGraw-Hill conference room. We all sat around a long, impressive, polished wood table. That is where Osborn Associates, after meticulous study, gave us their expert report. They announced that the evidence was "overwhelming" that all the documents were written by the same hand. The Osborns concluded that, "The chances of these documents being a forgery are one in a million." Loud applause from everyone at that long table. Now McGraw-Hill and LIFE had an unshakable guarantee that would hold up in court.

Unfortunately that one-in-a-million shot would come through.

We also got a different kind of expert opinion from

Frank McCulloch. He approached the Irving manuscript with profound skepticism, but his reading of it convinced him that it was authentic. This was the real Howard Hughes talking. And as further proof, Hughes had told Irving something previously said only to Frank himself in a long-ago *Time* file that had never been published. (Cliff no doubt photocopied that when I had let him read all our Hughes files.)

So how could we explain the outright denial from the voice that Frank identified as Howard Hughes? We came up with the only reasonable explanation. Hughes had been so outspoken that Chester Davis and other high-level Hughes executives persuaded their boss that the book could damage his vast business interests. Therefore he must deny it. Therefore he did.

We went merrily ahead. He had cashed our checks, the book was authentic. LIFE had excerpted three long articles and was ready to publish. Cliff, having recovered his cool, talked freely to reporters and survived his appearance on *60 Minutes* with Mike Wallace.

Coming up roses!

But two other investigations turned up ugly weeds.

The Credit Suisse bank, under heavy investigative pressure from us and from Swiss legal authorities, broke secrecy rules and admitted that the person who had opened the account and deposited the checks was a woman. At a Time Inc. executive meeting, after hearing this news, our president, James Shepley came up with an inspired explanation: "I bet it's Elmyr de Hory in drag!" But no, "H.R. Hughes," according to her forged passport, was Helga R. Hughes. And, again according to passport investigation, Helga R. Hughes, disguised in a wig and heavy makeup, turned out to be Cliff's wife, Edith Irving.

The second investigation, our search through air-line records and passenger manifests of Cliff's various trips to meet with Hughes, revealed that he had usually been accompanied by a lovely blonde cabaret singer named Nina Van Pallandt, who turned out to be his long-time mistress.

All right, *now* the jig is up, right? No, even now, no not quite.

The final memorable meeting around that McGraw Hill conference table took place when we at last knew that the book, which we had all read and enjoyed, was a fake. Albert Leventhal, the McGraw-Hill editor for trade books and boss of the Hughes book, came up with a possible escape hatch. He asked if any of us remembered a book called *Bridey Murphy,* which had been a smash-hit number one best seller as nonfiction. Then it turned out that *Bridey Murphy*, like the Hughes book, was a total fraud. "You know what happened?" Albert Leventhal asked us. "It just moved over to number one on the fiction best-seller list. Why don't we publish anyway?"

He had a splendid point because Irving's fake book was, in large part, good reading. With all the publicity, the fake book would have sold very well. I would love to have published the three excerpts we had created for LIFE, cheerfully admitting that we had bought a fake but isn't it great fun to read. But the Hughes lawyers would have enjoined any such publication.

In the end, of course, everybody lost. We all lost.

Clifford Irving and his wife, Edith, and his partner,

Richard Suskind, all went to jail. Everybody at McGraw-Hill and LIFE looked like fools, as indeed we were, me most of all. Day after day the investigation and the discoveries were on the front page of major newspapers and on TV. It was the top news story of the day, so the whole world knew how dumb we had been. The solitary winner was Nina van Pallandt. I put her on the cover of LIFE at the denouement, and the cover and the notoriety gave a brief boost to her cabaret career. Dave Maness and I had a lunch with her, and she told us that she had known from the very first trip to Mexico City that Cliff's project was a complete fraud. She, like Cliff, was charming company.

So everybody lost except Nina. But I have to say, fool though I was, that it was great fun. And Cliff himself writes at the end of his book *The Hoax*, "You want me to feel guilty? I don't. Because I enjoyed every goddam minute of it."

After Cliff pled guilty and was sentenced to prison in June 1972, I got a letter from a lawyer asking if I would be willing to write my support for a reduced sentence.

Back then I was still angry and embarrassed by all the anguish and humiliation he had caused all of us, very much including me personally. I threw the letter away. I have not seen or heard from Cliff since then.

But I wish now, all these years later, that I had given my support for a reduced sentence. He had, after all, given me and all the rest of us dupes a journalistic hayride that would be hard to beat.

I take my final ironic delight from Cliff's published comment on *The Hoax* movie.

He said it wasn't quite accurate.

OTHER GREATS

Bourke-White and Eisenstaedt were the most famous LIFE photographers, but many others were — in one way or another, or in many ways — outstanding.

I am neither a professional nor artistic critic of photography. I was a longtime working editor of a great picture magazine with a great staff of photographers. I dealt, week after week, year after year, with the work of all LIFE photographers. I constantly looked at their pictures and selected which ones should run in the magazine. But my views are those of working press, not critical scholarship.

Here are brief portraits of seven of these talented figures. I could easily have picked ten others — for instance, Carl Mydans, Nina Lean, George Silk, Ralph Morse, John Loengard, Dmitri Kessel, Mark Kaufman, Eliot Elisofon, Leonard McComb, Lennart Nilsson. Each of them took famous pictures and was renowned for some special achievement. Nilsson, a Swedish photographer who specialized in pictures *inside* the human body, shot the greatest color essay that ever ran in LIFE — and perhaps anywhere else. It was an April 1965 cover and sixteen inside pages called "Drama of Life Before Birth," a sequential picture of the way a baby develops from sperm and ovary to full-grown fetus.

Photojournalism aficionados will note that I have not

included Robert Capa. He was an incredibly brave man and a dashing, magnetic, colorful character. He took two great pictures: the soldier in the Spanish Civil War at the exact moment of his death by rifle fire, and the blurred images of the D-Day landing at Normandy, blurred not because Capa's pictures were out of focus but because a darkroom attendant in London had overheated Capa's film in the developing process so that only a handful of images survived. I wonder if those few images would have become so famous if they had *not* been blurred, and if there had been no legendary darkroom accident. Yes, Capa was out there in the Normandy surf *in advance* of the troops, and that alone is worthy of legend, but aside from the richly deserved legend we will never know how good the pictures were.

I give Capa credit for two great quotes. About combat photography he said, "If your pictures aren't good enough, it's because you're not close enough." And at the end of World War II when the German army was in collapse, he was invited to photograph the surrender of a German general. The Nazi general said to his American counterparts, in forceful German, "I am tired of all these photographers." Capa instantly answered in perfect German, "And I am tired of photographing all these defeated German generals."

The seven photographers I have chosen to write about were especially important, but we also shared personal experiences that I found particularly interesting.

LIFE photographers were intensely competitive, not only with each other but within themselves on each story assignment. Did I get the best picture? Did I just miss the perfect picture? Is this story going to make the magazine? Do I have a chance for a cover?

Because of the ferocious competition with each other and within themselves, they were often extremely difficult when they were out on a story. Reporters and correspondents often had to spend time soothing the offended subjects of the story, explaining that the photographer didn't really mean the terrible thing he just said, or that he didn't really mean to make that impossible request.

A LIFE photographer on a major assignment could be hard to live with. Not all of them, and not all the time. But many of them, and often.

GENE SMITH

Many people — scholars, critics, serious LIFE editors — would vote Gene Smith the greatest LIFE photographer. I do not. I do think he was the greatest creator of black-and-white essays, perhaps LIFE's most important photographic invention.

The black-and-white essay, a story told in pictures over eight or ten pages, got better and better through the years, and Gene Smith's essays were the very best. Spanish Village. The Midwife. Dr. Schweitzer. The Minamata Chemical Disaster. And my own favorite as LIFE's best black-and-white essay ever, Country Doctor. He often worked alone, in faraway places, in total control of his story from start to finish. At least in control until he handed in his film, at which point an editor and an art director chose the pictures and made the layout. At which point Gene was often disappointed and highly argumentative over the result. Everybody else was always impressed by his pictures and story.

Without taking any credit away from this achievement, I think Gene Smith was the most tortured, most impossible photographer on the staff. He grandly quit the staff in protest over some moralistic issue, declaring his own monumental integrity and independence. He became, and remains, a sainted figure in the world of photography. He then spent the remaining years of his life, impoverished and in poor health, cadging free film and camera equipment and camera repairs and other benefits from the magazine he had so eloquently denounced.

As a young reporter, I spent one week with Gene Smith traveling around the country to explore a story that not only never ran but was never even shot. The subject was the Adolescent Boy. My editor, John Dille, Sociology Department, had sent a query to bureaus and stringers describing the kind of boy we were looking for to be the subject of an essay on the trials and pleasures and troubles of a teenager's life. The query described what was wanted quite thoroughly, but I still remember Dille's absurd little point that, for photographic reasons, "He should not have pimples, but his friends can have pimples." The bureaus and stringers sent in their nominations, Dille and I narrowed them down to half a dozen possibilities in three different cities, and Gene Smith and I took off to look at them, talk to them and then pick the winner.

Gene was physically unimpressive, middle height, frail build, slightly bald, glasses, nondescript clothes. Everything was in his personality, nothing in his appearance. During our travels and meals together he was good company, not fun but interesting. As a World War II correspondent he had been wounded in the mouth by shrapnel, and he talked about his long, agonizing recovery. He said the wound still bothered him, I think perhaps more psychologically than physically. He still took a lot of pills.

When it came to our interviews with each of the candidates, either at the boy's school or at his home, Gene sat off to the side and let me ask the questions and carry on the conversation. He would watch each boy, expressions, gestures, thinking how he would look in pictures. He occasionally took a quick candid as a picture reminder, but mostly he listened. At the end of each session when Gene and I were safely alone, he explained why this boy would not do. I don't remember his reasons, but there was always something. I thought one or two boys were quite possible, but the photographer has the controlling vote.

Finally, in New Orleans, the last boy on our list, Gene thought this was a possibility — the only possibility. *Maybe* this boy might make a story. But it turned out that the boy attended a Catholic parochial high school, a special situation, not the kind of all-American high school that our all-American adolescent boy should attend.

During our trip Gene introduced me to two things I have since enjoyed, New Orleans jazz and brandy alexanders.

After our report, John Dille decided that we should drop this story idea. I wondered, and still wonder today, if Gene had deliberately or even subconsciously picked the only boy that would not fit the proposed story. Maybe he just didn't like the story.

Or maybe something else. Who knows? With Gene Smith you never knew.

I have said I don't think he was our greatest photographer, even though he shot some of our very greatest stories. I think he was limited by his own intransigence. He never bothered to shoot color, even after color pages became widely available. As an assignment editor I would never have trusted him to shoot a news story, a sports story, an entertainment story, a fashion story, a food story — or really anything else except his own intense specialty, the human-interest story. As a photographer on a far-ranging picture magazine that needed good pictures in many areas, he was a brilliant and tragic luxury.

DAVE DUNCAN

In any photographer poll the overwhelming winners for Most Glamorous would have been: Woman: Margaret Bourke-White. Man: David Douglas Duncan.

Dave Duncan was not just glamorous — a couple of inches over six feet, dark-haired, strikingly handsome, very masculine — but a wonderful and dashing photographer. A great war photographer, he shot the Marines' deadly, bitter-cold Christmas retreat from Changjin Reservoir in the Korean War and the vivid siege of Khe-Sanh in the Vietnam War. A Marine himself in World War II, he knew war and soldiers, and he was a superb combat photographer — better than the more famous Robert Capa.

Duncan, like Gene Smith, resigned from the LIFE staff on principles of independence but, unlike Smith, he was a great success as a freelance. He became a neighbor and close friend of Pablo Picasso in France and did several good books on the artist's private life. These books are probably the finest photographic record of a great artist at work and at play.

Duncan was also, unlike most photographers, a shrewd businessman. Very early in his freelance career he discovered that he could create his own photographic books in full color at very low cost and very high quality

in Japan and Hong Kong. This is a photographer's dream:
I choose my own pictures, I make my own layouts, I write
my own captions and text, and I then own the book and
all its profits.

Even after his resignation from our staff, Duncan was
willing to take on a good LIFE assignment. Or to bring in
a good idea of his own. My happiest example came in
April 1971 while I was managing editor. Dave walked
into my office to tell me that he had just seen a radical
new musical. He was so impressed that he went back a
second time to take pictures. He predicted that this would
turn out to be a breakthrough show when it got to Broadway, and here was a chance for LIFE to introduce it for
the first time to American readers.

He showed me his black-and-white performance pictures and told me the story of the play and its songs. I,
too, was impressed. The pictures were excellent, and although I had not heard any of the music, I trusted Dave's
enthusiasm. On May 5, six months before it opened on
Broadway, we ran a cover and a lead story on Andrew
Lloyd Webber's first great hit, *Jesus Christ, Superstar.*

GJON MILI

Mili was as much an engineer as a photographer. In fact, he was trained as an engineer in his native Albania, and when he came to America he worked closely with MIT Professor Harold Edgerton, a pioneer in flash photography. Together they perfected multiple strobe flash, and Mili used this technique for many of his best-known photographs. My own favorite is his recreation of Marcel Duchamp's *Nude Descending a Staircase*. Mili's nude is endlessly repeated by stroboscopic flash as she walks downstairs, the images overlapping. I like the photograph better than the painting because it is sharper, brighter and more sensual. Not worth as much, however.

He was not just a cold technician. He loved jazz and ballet. He shot a very jazzy repetitive-strobe-flash picture of Benny Goodman's great drummer Gene Krupa in action, drumsticks flashing all over the place. Late in his career he photographed a ballet performance in color with strobe lighting, creating beautiful, soft, impressionistic pictures of motion.

The story on which Mili and I had the closest contact did not involve strobe lights.

To Mili's dismay, he was not allowed to use any artificial light of any kind and had to shoot the entire color essay by natural light — of which there was very little.

The story was Chartres Cathedral. I of course knew it existed and had seen a few pictures, but when my wife and I visited Chartres during a trip through France, we were overwhelmed by its dark and monumental beauty. Back in New York, I discovered that LIFE had never done a big picture story on Chartres and immediately got it assigned. I was surprised the story was given to Mili, since no strobe lighting would be involved, but he told me he had himself long admired Chartres and had begged for the story.

Gjon was a tall, shaggy man with a bristly gray mustache. He had black-rimmed glasses that he wore far down on his nose. Peering over these glasses gave him a skeptical look.

It turned out that he had every right to be skeptical about Chartres because the cathedral refused to let him use any artificial light whatsoever, not even the tiniest flash bulb, not even an ordinary lightbulb. To introduce light of any kind would, said the authorities, disturb the serenity of worship. The cathedral, which was actually very pleased about this big LIFE story, did allow Mili to use a tripod so that, with his lens wide open, he could take extra long exposures in the dark interior without his camera moving in his hands. The only light available came through the gorgeous stained glass windows and the many candles. The only easy pictures, Gjon told me when he came back to New York, were of the windows themselves and of the altar area illumined by countless candles.

Then, with particular reverence, he showed me his favorite picture of the entire set. It was a dark picture, like so many of the others. It showed, in middle distance, a beautiful seated nun, in profile, rapt in prayer. I could barely see her in that quiet darkness but, perhaps because of that cathedral darkness, it was a strangely moving photograph.

I congratulated him.

Mili shook his head. "Don't congratulate me. This picture cannot be taken."

I asked what he meant.

"It is technically impossible. There was not enough light. I saw her sitting there, and she looked so perfect, but it was so dark. I couldn't take a long exposure because if she moved even slightly, she would become a blur. I just held the camera as steady as I could, took a deep breath to hold myself steady, and shot it." He pointed down to the light table, to this picture. "One exposure. There was no way it would come out."

"But it's here. It did come out."

Gjon looked at me over those glasses, far down his nose. He could not have been more solemn, more serious, less skeptical.

"Not my doing," he said. "I couldn't have done it." He shrugged. "It was just meant to be."

GORDON PARKS

Gordon Parks was the only black photographer on LIFE. Not just somewhat black but very black — dark, dark brown skin. He was the closest thing we had to a Renaissance man, not just on LIFE but in all of Time Inc. The camera was only one of his tools. He wrote books, including a brilliant autobiographical novel called *The Learning Tree.*

As the first black director for a major studio, he turned the novel into a movie — with himself as coproducer, director, screenplay writer and composer of the music. He also wrote and directed the successful movie *Shaft* and its sequels, featuring a flashy, sexy black detective who got off many jibes at whites. He also composed classical music, which was performed at Carnegie Hall. There seemed to be nothing he couldn't do — except one thing. In the LIFE photo lab, where he was very popular, hung a huge, smiling portrait of Gordon with the mocking black caption, "I don't do windows."

This is not about his other achievements but only about his work as a photographer.

Born dirt poor in rural Kansas, youngest of fifteen children, after a miserable and hazardous childhood, he managed to scrabble his way into photography, using a $12.50 camera he bought in a pawnshop. He was just good enough and more than ambitious enough to be hired during the Depression by Roy Stryker, who developed many young photographers from the unlikely setting of the Farm Security Administration in Washington, D.C. There, as a young and not very experienced photographer, Gordon shot his most famous picture. It is an elderly black charwoman, Ella Watson, her face bleak and blank, staring straight into the camera, holding a mop and broom and standing in front of an American flag. He called it "American Gothic, Washington, D.C." When Gordon died in 2006 at ninety-three, this was the picture that appeared in every newspaper and on every TV news broadcast. It is a perfect picture, packed with emotion and thought and social impact. I always meant to ask Gordon how he felt about the fact that his most famous picture was taken at the very beginning of his career before he had even begun to do his greatest picture stories. I never got around to asking, but I still wonder.

As the one and only black photographer on an all-white, immensely popular magazine, Gordon enjoyed many unique advantages. He could do stories in the black world that no white photographer could possibly do. His first great essay for LIFE was the story of a young Harlem gang leader named Red Jackson. LIFE's editors and LIFE's readers had never seen such a story inside the black world. During the civil rights movement of the sixties, Gordon was able to do stories on the Black Muslims, the Black Panthers and the revolutionary leader Malcolm X. They all wanted LIFE's giant publicity for their cause, but Gordon was the only photographer they trusted to tell it right.

While he was working on his Malcolm X story, Gordon paid me an enormous compliment, although I did not realize at the time the risk he was taking. Because I would be the top editor on the story, Gordon brought Malcolm X to my office for a half-hour talk. He was a memorable figure, tall, handsome, light-skinned, wearing glasses, intellectual, eloquent and, above all, cool. Our talk was serious but pleasant, quite easy for both of us. The risk, I now realize, was that Malcolm might have disliked me or mistrusted me, or that I might have inadvertently said something that wrecked Gordon's story. I guess I behaved all right, because Malcolm X went on with the story, and it ran in the magazine at substantial length.

Gordon's most powerful and popular essay was not about blacks, although it might as well have been. It was the story of Flavio, a young, asthmatic boy who lived in a slum called the *favela* in Rio de Janieiro. In spite of his youth and his health — he was close to dying — Flavio took care of his whole family. Gordon's pictures provoked a national outpouring of sympathy and financial contributions from our readers, enough to bring Flavio to America for expert and lifesaving medical treatment.

But Gordon was not a narrow heart-and-soul photographer like Gene Smith.

He was also a magnificent color fashion photographer, and he once shot a smashing color essay of great food markets all over the world.

Gordon was, not surprisingly, a good friend of Muhammad Ali and took many pictures of that great heavyweight champion, including several covers. Gordon's and my only serious disagreement over the many years we had known each other was about an Ali picture — or rather a non-picture.

At the first Ali-Frazier championship fight in Madison Square Garden, Ali took a physical beating during the biggest defeat of his long career. His beautiful face, of which he had been so vociferously proud, was bruised, puffed up, banged up. In his dressing room after the fight, he allowed no photographers — except his personal friend Gordon Parks.

As Gordon told me the next day, Ali said through his swollen lips, "Well, Gordon, I suppose you're going to take a picture of me looking like this." Obviously Ali was expecting and permitting this.

"No, Champ," Gordon said. "I'm not going to take any pictures."

I was outraged. "You can't not take that picture."

"He's my friend."

I told Gordon I didn't care. He was a journalist. He *had* to take that picture. It was an exclusive news opportunity, an exclusive human opportunity. He *had* to shoot it. He could then suppress it if he wanted to, he could avoid telling me that he had taken the picture, he could release it weeks or months later if he chose to. Or he could even hold it back forever. But he had to take the picture.

More than thirty years later I still believe that.

Gordon just repeated, "He's my friend."

JOHN DOMINIS

I often said, and still say today, that if I had to start a picture magazine with a single photographer, I would choose John Dominis. He was neither as famous as others nor as outstanding in this field or that field, but he could shoot everything. He was equally skilled in black-and-white and color. He was expert at lighting. He was a sports photographer, a nature photographer, a news photographer, a food photographer, a war photographer, a people photographer.

And he had one other qualification that would be invaluable if, as an editor, you had only one photographer on your new picture magazine. He was a really nice guy. Everybody liked him. He did not sulk. He was not temperamental. He liked to work. He was fun to be with, whether he was working or playing. You don't get too many of those in the ranks of professional photographers.

I worked with Dominis a lot, partly in the field, on stories but mostly as an editor in New York. In the l950s, I was Chicago bureau chief and John was the top bureau photographer. We went out on stories together, but we also spent a lot of social and drinking time together in Chicago. By happenstance, it was an especially convivial bureau. The correspondents and photographers and various wives and girlfriends and boyfriends spent many evenings together, with considerable drinking and singing and competitive performances, late in the evening, of the ski exercise and the Coke bottle exercise. I will not describe these athletic ferocities beyond saying that Dominis was especially good at them. He had spent his California teenage years as a passionate surfboarder, and as an end he played in the Rose Bowl for Southern Cal. He was just under six feet, very good-looking, always in good physical shape, many smiles and laughs.

Back in New York, after our Chicago hiatus, John did many stories for me in the nature field and many food stories for my wife, Eleanor, in her Great Dinners series that ran every month for five years. He took both the best animal picture and the best food picture that LIFE ever ran.

The food picture first. Until Eleanor's Great Dinners, most food pictures in magazines, newspapers and books showed food on dining room tables in elaborate place settings — china, silver, glassware. Eleanor chose to show the food itself in a single dramatic picture filling a LIFE spread. She deliberately used only photographers who loved food and who had never before taken food pictures. John Dominis shot more of these than anyone else.

Their greatest triumph was trout amandine. Since trout leap, and since lightly browned almonds are beautiful, they came up with the idea of showing a perfectly sautéed trout leaping out of a deep bed of almonds. This required putting a hook inside the trout, attached by a wire. When John was camera ready, an assistant yanked the wire, and the trout leapt out and upward, accompanied by a trail of almonds. Unfortunately, when the wire was pulled, the cooked trout fell apart in midair. Much dismay, many experiments, a certain amount of tension. The final solution, after many failed attempts involving many trout, was to sauté the trout with the hook and wire already attached inside, then put it in a freezer until it was rock solid.

The final picture that ran in the magazine was, Eleanor remembers, only the fourth or fifth in her monthly series. It was an absolute breakthrough food picture, action caught in midair, leaping trout and leaping almonds, nothing like it ever seen before. It could have been taken by a sports photographer — as indeed it was.

John was the best animal photographer I ever worked with, and I had worked with many. Soon after I became a writer, I was given the Nature Department. I knew nothing about nature, but the LIFE theory was to hire bright writers and then assume, sometimes erroneously, that they could learn to do more or less anything. I learned to love nature stories, especially the animals. As I rose through the ranks, I made sure that the Nature Department always reported to me.

Patricia Hunt, who had been my researcher and then my successor as nature editor, brought me the idea of doing a grand series of color essays on what she called The Great Cats of Africa. John got the assignment and spent most of the next year in Africa photographing lions, leopards and cheetahs. The three resulting long color essays were filled with great pictures that were later published as a book. The greatest single picture — in my opinion the greatest animal picture I have ever seen — shows a leopard about to kill a baboon who has turned back toward his pursuer in last-second desperation.

Lions and cheetahs are, relatively, quite available for

pictures. Leopards are not. Leopards are more solitary, more hidden. In order to get his leopard-baboon picture, John had to do two things for which purists vigorously attacked him when the story was published. To get his leopard essay, he had to rent two half-wild leopards from an African animal keeper. And he had to release captive baboons in the leopards' presence.

Therefore, said the purists, this is a set-up picture and a fake.

I agree that there is much to be said for this position. Yes indeed, it is a picture set up by the photographer. Yes indeed, this picture was not taken "in the wild." But there is nothing fake about the picture itself. That is a real leopard. That is a real baboon. And they are vividly captured in their very real final moment.

John and I still see each other in New York City. The most regular occasion is our annual Chinese New Year's dinner at Shun Lee West. We always have this feast with another LIFE couple, Roy and Helen Rowan, who spent years in our Hong Kong bureau. Eleanor and I have ourselves been to China, but our better claim to the China Card is that we helped found and then ate often at Pearl's popular Chinese restaurant. John's longtime girlfriend, Anne Hollister, is a superb LIFE researcher, but she is the only one of us who has no China claims.

Ordinarily, if you have so many old China hands at a dinner, the opportunities for dispute over the menu are unlimited. But by unanimous consent the feast, seven or eight courses, is ordered ahead of time by Dominis. The dinner is always a success. And he is still a really nice guy.

PHILIPPE HALSMAN

Halsman was the ultimate studio photographer. He had a giant studio where he could control everything: lights, backgrounds, stage settings for his pictures. His assistant was his wife, Yvonne, who was expert at controlling and soothing his subjects and, when necessary, controlling and soothing Philippe himself who, like most photographers, had a temperamental streak.

Philippe was primarily a cover photographer and an extremely good one. When I became managing editor, I received a poignant letter from Philippe. He had had himself photographed surrounded by his ninety-nine LIFE covers spread out on the floor around him. He asked — no, begged — to be assigned number one hundred. He finally got it on January 23, 1970, with Johnny Carson, an unmatched number of covers.

His most famous picture, however, was not a cover. It was a crazy studio creation of the mad artist Salvador Dali, leaping in midair, pretending to paint a picture, while three cats are hurled toward him, along with a lot of hurled water. There is also, in case you think there is not enough going on, a straight-backed chair hanging in midair. The picture took forever since it required throwing cats and water over and over again, while Dali leapt and leapt, until Halsman got the image he wanted.

But back to real life. Philippe got the idea that, at the end of each studio portrait session, he would ask his subjects if they would be willing, just for fun, to take off their shoes and let him take a picture of them jumping. Almost everybody said yes, eventually resulting in *Jump Book*. The best-known results are Marilyn Monroe and the Duke and Duchess of Windsor.

As a young reporter in 1949, I worked with Philippe for several weeks on an elaborate portrait essay for LIFE's Mid-Century Issue. Our subject was famous figures from the 1920s. Most of these — Nobel novelist Sinclair Lewis, cartoonist John Held, Jr., movie actress Clara Bow, New York City greeter Grover Whalen — could be photographed under optimum conditions — i.e., in Philippe's own studio with wife Yvonne as super assistant. But two of them — dancer Gilda Gray (inventor of the scandalous Shimmy, and played by Rita Hayworth in the movie *Gilda*) and John Scopes, the accused teacher of evolution in the famous "Monkey Trial" — had to be photographed out of town on location.

I found Gilda Gray in Denver. She sounded delightful over the phone. She said she still had her old costume and, though now in her fifties, could still fit into it. But she no longer had her silver dancing slippers. She described them, silver straps that ran partway up her legs, gave me her shoe size and told me where I could buy them in Manhattan.

I found John Scopes in Baton Rouge, Louisiana. Over the phone he sounded a lot less interesting than Gilda Gray, which proved to be the case.

Forced out of his beloved studio for these two portraits, Philippe came up with two ideas. He would photograph Gilda from a great distance in a huge ball-room. Her tiny figure, spotlighted in this cavernous half-dark setting would emphasize the nostalgic distance from her days of fame. I thought a sexy dancer who could still fit into her sexy costume, silver slippers and all, was worth a sexy close-up, but the photographer is king. I got a list of Denver ballrooms so that Philippe could pick the one he wanted when we got there.

For Scopes, whose old newspaper pictures looked quite bland, Philippe wanted props that would shout evo-lution. I was instructed to find busts or small statues of an ape, a gorilla and an early man, then ship them to Baton Rouge. Yes, I actually found and rented three such busts from Columbia University and paid to have them shipped in a barrel to our Baton Rouge stringer, who would hold them for our arrival.

Off we flew to Denver with Philippe's suitcases of camera equipment and lights and Gilda's silver slippers. Yvonne did not like to travel, so Philippe brought along a young man to be his assistant. Philippe at that time was in his mid-forties. A bit below average height, slightly balding, he wore black horn-rimmed glasses. He consid-ered himself an elitist, a cultured European man of the world, as indeed he was.

As soon as we had checked in, we set out to choose a ballroom. I had four of them lined up, every giant hotel ballroom in Denver. Philippe liked the very first one he saw and told me to reserve it for tomorrow. I did. Philippe then said we might as well look at the others in case they were better. Off to the second, which he thought was slightly better than the first and told me to reserve it. I did. Same result with the third, and then the fourth. By the time we had finished, no one could have given a dance in Denver the next day without buying a ballroom from LIFE.

Philippe and his assistant finally settled on the third ballroom because it offered the best shooting angle from the balcony and because it had the best lighting, requiring only a spotlight or two from Philippe's collection to highlight Gilda. I released the other three ballrooms so that Denver's social life could continue.

Gilda arrived for her performance right on time, wearing sneakers and wrapped in a raincoat. She had short dyed hair, a great smile, a lively sense of what fun this was going to be. When she took off her raincoat, it was instantly obvious that she could still fit into her old costume — low-cut bosom, short skirt, lots of spangles against a black background. Philippe, a devotee of sexual splendor in women, was as impressed as I was. His lower lip came out in his characteristic gesture of approval. I think he was beginning to wonder about that long-distance shot from the balcony. I gave Gilda her silver dancing slippers, which fit perfectly, and she was set to go.

Philippe explained his thinking about the balcony shot. He didn't sound too convincing, or too convinced, about his own plan, but Gilda said anything he wanted was fine with her. "Just tell me when to dance."

Philippe took half a dozen shots from the balcony, explaining to me what a creative idea this was. He told Gilda — shouted down to her — that he did not want her actively dancing, just take a suggestive pose. When he had finished his balcony work, he then casually said, "As long as we're here, I think I will take a few close-ups."

So Philippe and his assistant and I and all the camera equipment moved down from the balcony to the dance floor and shot Gilda, silver-slippered, bare-legged, smiling, sexy and up close.

That is the picture that ran in the magazine

Kris Kristofferson's great song *Me and Bobby McGee*, made world famous by Janis Joplin, opens with the phrase "Busted flat in Baton Rouge." It was the very worst predicament Kristofferson could think of.

John Scopes wasn't busted flat, but he lived alone in a dreary Baton Rouge rooming house. I visited him there to say hello, tell him what to wear (jacket and tie) and where to meet us for tomorrow's shoot. He was a tall, very quiet man, receding hair, colorless rimmed glasses and colorless, unexpressive face and personality. It was hard to believe that this former biology teacher had once been the focus of a nation-gripping trial about evolution, featuring William Jennings Bryan and Clarence Darrow, later turned into a dramatic play and movie called *Inherit the Wind*.

I reported back to Philippe that Scopes himself was not going to make a good picture. I congratulated him on thinking up the ape busts, and then I set off to find them.

I checked our hotel desk for a message from our stringer. Yes, here it was: the barrel of busts had arrived safely, a schoolroom with a long table, as requested, was reserved for us at such-and-such address. The stringer was sorry to miss all the fun, including the pleasure of watching a famous LIFE photographer at work, but he was off to Texas to see the big Louisiana State football game. No mention of where the barrel of ape busts might be.

I spent a dozen desperate hours trying to find the barrel. I checked our own hotel, I checked other hotels, I checked the school, I checked the stringer's newspaper, I tried to check his home and his office, but no answer. In those days, no cell phones. Everywhere I called, everywhere I went, I asked the same idiotic question, "Do you have a barrel of ape busts for LIFE Magazine?"

Next morning, Saturday, the day of our shoot and the day of the LSU game, I was still searching. I had an insane vision of paging the stringer at the stadium and asking him to call at once. Philippe and his assistant went to the schoolroom to be ready to meet Scopes and, if necessary, to shoot him without any props, a deplorable prospect.

Having exhausted every other possibility I could think of, I decided I had to get into the stringer's office, which was in a separate building from his newspaper. Maybe he had left the barrel there with instructions to an assistant or a secretary or a janitor to get in touch with me, or to tell me when I phoned, and that somehow this planned connection had failed.

I went by taxi to the office building. It was closed for the weekend, but two guards were on duty. I explained what I was looking for, absurd as that might sound, and why they had to let me in. No dice without the stringer's permission. I explained where the stringer was, unreachable in some seat in some stadium in Texas. Still no dice.

So I made them a bet. If the barrel wasn't in the stringer's office, I would give them $25, a fair sum in 1949. And if the barrel *was* there, I would pay them $50 to open the barrel, unload the contents and help me into a taxi. Money talks, especially on a boring Saturday. We took the elevator, they opened the office door, and there

sat the barrel, clearly labeled for LIFE. Hammers and
screwdrivers, splintered wood, a lot of protective straw
packing, and $50 later, plus taxi fare, I arrived at the
scene.

The scene was pitiful. There stood Philippe and his
assistant and the cameras, and there on the long wooden
table was a scraggly stuffed monkey, hanging by one arm
from the limb of a patently fake tree. Philippe, as desperate as I to find a prop, any prop, had looked up "Taxi-
dermist" in the phone book and rented this shabby
creature, whose stuffing was hanging out of his armpit.

Busted flat in Baton Rouge.

The assistant and I carried the ape busts to the table
and set them in a chronological row. The monkey, relieved
of his task to represent Darwin and evolution, was hidden
away out of sight. John Scopes arrived, was seated, ex-
pressionless, at the end of the table with the ape busts
ranged in front of him, and Philippe shot his picture.

It actually ran in the magazine.

The three of us went to New Orleans for our flight home
to New York. Our work was done, we had our pictures,
and it was time to celebrate. Philippe, the cosmopolitan
expert, knew exactly what to do. Dinner at Antoine's —
with Philippe as our host and guide. *Host* is misleading,
since of course this was on Philippe's LIFE expense account, but *guide* is correct. Philippe ordered every drink
and every dish, for which his assistant and I were most
grateful since the elaborate menu was far beyond our understanding.

All through the long, delicious dinner Philippe entertained us by asking acute, cultured questions of our

waiter. "How do you make the *pommes soufflé*? What is Antione's most popular dish?" On and on, straight through, he was showing off his epicurean expertise, not only to his assistant and me but also to the waiter.

At the end, the waiter invited us to take a tour of the dining room because there were many interesting plaques on the walls, with entertaining tidbits from Antoine's long and colorful history. So we took the tour, reading plaque after plaque. I remember one about Teddy Roosevelt's visit when he pronounced his dinner "Dee-licious!" But the plaque that most caught the attention of all three of us, especially Philippe, was the list of "The Ten Questions Most Frequently Asked at Antoine's." Poor Philippe, cultural impressario, had asked every single one of them.

LIFE's Mid-Century Issue was a success, and Philippe's pictures ran for ten pages in color, the best and biggest story in the magazine.

Gilda Gray had given me back the silver slippers, saying that at her age she had no more use for them. "Give them to a pretty girl."

I gave them to a pretty LIFE colleague named Eleanor Parish, who happened to be the same shoe size. I later married her. I don't think there was any direct cause-and-effect connection, but you never know.

LARRY BURROWS

All during the Vietnam War we kept thinking up assignments that would take Larry Burrows away from his war. Not just little itty-bitty assignments for a day or two but long, difficult ones that would keep him out of harm's way for weeks at a time. Birds of Paradise. The Taj Mahal. He did them and did them superbly, then went right back to his war.

In the end we did not succeed. In February 1971 he was killed, along with several other journalists, in a helicopter crash over Laos. Our military flew over the crash site, saw the wreckage and said no one had survived. It would be many years before the site could be visited and the remains identified and recovered. Larry had always said that what he most wanted to do was to photograph Vietnam at peace. He didn't make it.

I was managing editor when the news came through. After the initial shock, I decided that I should fly to Hong Kong for Larry's funeral service. It may have been the most popular decision I made during my four years as M.E. Many staff members told me afterward that my gesture had made them proud of their magazine. I didn't do it for the magazine, I did it for Larry. I wrote in my weekly Editor's Note that, without prejudice against anybody else, Larry Burrows was "the single bravest and most dedicated war photographer I know of." I still think so.

He was a tall, vigorous man, several inches over six feet. He was British, and he wore glasses, even in combat. He spent nine years covering the war, often at huge personal risk. Between battles and raids and air strikes and combat missions, he also shot heartbreaking essays on the Vietnamese children, whom he saw as the deepest casualties of war. There was a boy named Lao, on crutches, and a lovely young girl named Tranh, who was getting an artificial leg. After fifty years I may have misremembered their names, but I have not forgotten their pictures.

I have said that I thought Gene Smith's "Country Doctor" was LIFE's finest black-and-white essay. But it is important to realize that Smith had weeks to do that story. He could pick his own moments, his own sites for pictures. He could wait and wait for the right event to happen, for just the right picture to tell his story. He had all the time in the world.

Larry Burrows shot LIFE's greatest live-action essay in a single day, in a handful of hours under violent combat conditions. It is the story of a very young Marine crew chief, Lance Corporal James Farley, the machine gunner on a helicopter called *Yankee Papa 13*. Larry had no control over the story except his own skill and bravery, and his quickness and experience as a combat photographer. He could only shoot what was happening right now.

The story opens with a jaunty, smiling Farley walking out to his helicopter carrying his two machine guns. *Yankee Papa 13*, along with other helicopters, is assigned to deliver a battalion of Vietnamese infantry to an area controlled by the Viet Cong. From just inside the copter door, Larry has a vivid action shot of helmeted Vietnamese soldiers leaping out into a high-grass field, with two other hovering helicopters in the distance, performing the same mission.

There is a lot of gunfire. Another copter, *Yankee Papa 3*, is shot down by heavy Viet Cong fire. Farley runs across the field under fire to help his comrades — and Larry runs with him to get his pictures. The pilot of *YP 3* is dead, but the wounded are helped into *YP 13*.

When Farley's copter finally lifts off to return to base, it carries one dead body and two wounded men — and Farley then discovers to his horror that his machine gun is jammed and he cannot defend his plane or his wounded. Burrows has a perfect picture of this specific second.

Yankee Papa 13 makes it home, with eleven bullet holes and the radio knocked out. Farley makes his report and then collapses, head down on his arms. Larry's story ends with that moment, in perfect contrast to the opening picture of the cheerful young Farley heading off to war.

Once when he was briefly back in New York on home leave, three LIFE friends took him to lunch in a Manhattan restaurant. Vietnam was going very badly, and there seemed to be no possible way out. After discussing the dismal situation, Larry, being British, said, "Well, thank God it's not my war."

One of his friends refused to let him get away with this. "Larry, if it isn't your war, whose is it?"

V-J Day, Times Square
by Alfred Eisenstaedt

Rita Hayworth by Bob Landry

American Gothic, Washington, D.C.
by Gordon Parks

Country Doctor
by W. Eugene Smith

Yankee Papa 13
by Larry Burrows

The Monkey in the Water
by Hansel Mieth

Buna Beach by George Strock

Yes, it was very much his war — and finally his death. He was just under forty-five when he was shot down over Laos. I think that if he had lived and gone on working, he might have become the greatest of all LIFE photographers. But, of course, that is only speculation.

MY EXCLUSIVE WITH GARBO

As a young LIFE reporter, I once had an exclusive interview with Greta Garbo when a dozen older, tougher, more experienced New York City newspaper reporters were unable to get a single word out of her.

Garbo was the most beautiful star in Hollywood — and the most inaccessible to the press. No interviews, no pictures, no nothing. Even though she had stopped making movies, her reclusiveness — and her beauty — remained a perpetual challenge to reporters and photographers. Nevertheless, for our Mid-Century Issue story on great figures of the twenties, I was asked to inveigle Garbo into coming to Philippe Halsman's studio and posing for pictures. I was *asked* to do this, but nobody expected me to succeed. However, because of LIFE's enormous reputation in those glory days of 1949, there was always a fighting chance if, somehow, I could only get word to her.

I got my chance when we learned that Garbo was coming home from Europe on some ocean liner. I could go out to the liner before passengers disembarked and, with luck, talk to her. The News Department, which knew how to arrange such things, got me a press pass on the little boat that was going out. Unfortunately, a dozen newspaper reporters and a few photographers also got press passes and were on the same boat. They all knew each other and they all talked about capturing the elusive Garbo. Obviously the odds against me had just risen higher. With all these people planning to badger her, how could I put in a civilized request for a studio appointment?

On board the liner the reporters tipped a steward to tell them Garbo's cabin number. We all trooped down to her cabin, which was at the end of a long, narrow corridor. Unfortunately for the cause, also standing at the end of this corridor, blocking Garbo's door, was a tall, dark-haired, middle-aged figure whose name I have forgotten but whom the reporters recognized as a Garbo friend. Was he more than a friend? While he blocked the way against the clamoring reporters, a tiny wizened woman reporter (what used to be called a sob sister) clung to his arm and kept asking, "Are you her paramour? Are you her paramour?" It is a quote that, spoken in dead earnest, I simply cannot forget, although I would never use it in a novel because we all know that real people don't talk like that. The friend (paramour?) stood steadfast.

A higher-ranking steward in a uniform with much gold braid appeared at the rear of our group and called out that he had an important and helpful suggestion for us. "Step back here with me." We all turned back to listen. Miss Garbo, he said, must go through the liner's customs desk and show her passport, just like every other passenger. She could not escape this. If we reporters followed him to the customs desks, we could not miss her. Since the friend/paramour was immovable, the herd of reporters took the steward's advice, and we followed him to the customs area.

A large open space with three desks in a row was occupied by three officials. Passengers in three lines waited with their passports in hand. The reporters took positions and waited for Garbo to appear.

Except for me. If I stayed with that bunch, I would never have a chance. But since I now knew where Garbo's cabin was, I would write her a letter and slip it under her door. If the guardian was still on watch, I would explain the situation to him and politely ask him to give Garbo my letter.

I had no trouble finding one of those little table-desks loaded with ship's stationery. I sat down and, as quickly as possible, wrote out my message. A bit complicated because I had to say "LIFE . . . special Mid-Century Issue . . . great figures of the 1920s, of which she was of course the greatest . . . studio of Philippe Halsman, who was of course the greatest photographer . . . blah, blah, blah . . . my phone number, Halsman's phone number . . . Most Sincerely." No time to edit or rewrite, must hurry, I sealed the envelope, wrote "Miss Garbo" on the front, underlined it and hurried back to her cabin.

To my surprise there was nobody in the long, narrow corridor, and — an even bigger surprise — her cabin door was open. I knocked. No answer. I knocked again. Same result.

I knew what to do. I stepped into the cabin, saw a small glass coffee table with flowers on it. I placed my "Miss Garbo" envelope on the table where, if she came back, she could not miss it. She would at least read it, wouldn't she? Anyway, I had done my best.

I stepped out of her cabin into the corridor.

I heard the tramp of many approaching feet. I heard approaching loud cries.

A figure, head down, came running toward me down the corridor.

One of the reporters later explained to me what had happened. He was still fuming about the perfidy of that high-ranking steward who must have been handsomely tipped by Garbo or her friend. Garbo did *not* go through the passenger passport line as the steward had promised. Instead, they snuck her in *behind* the customs desks and quickly stamped her passport for entry into the U.S. Even though she was wearing a broad-brimmed hat, one of the reporters recognized her just as she turned away.

"There she is!" he shouted and started toward her. The rest followed. She began running to escape. The reporters ran after her, the whole hungry crowd, all yelling, "Miss Garbo! Miss Garbo!"

She was trying to get back to her cabin before they caught up with her. In that narrow corridor, only a few steps from her open cabin door and safety, head down, Greta Garbo ran smack into me.

Suddenly blocked, she stepped back and raised her head. At a distance of no more than two feet the most beautiful face in the world glared at me. She gave me perhaps five seconds to appreciate that face. Then with her right arm, a surprisingly powerful right arm, she slammed me aside and cried, using the French pronunciation, "*Pardon!*"

She swept past, into her cabin, closing and locking the door behind her.

It could not be called a great interview, but I was the only reporter she spoke to that entire day. I have no idea if she ever read my letter, but she certainly did not answer it.

For the movie star in our twenties' portraits, we settled for Clara Bow.

EDITING GREAT WRITERS

In my thirty-five years at Time Inc. I held many jobs. My favorite was neither managing editor of LIFE nor editorial director of the whole company, although those were the highest rank, highest authority and highest pay. The best was articles editor of LIFE. Although we were primarily a picture magazine, we published many articles. Each week as articles editor I was responsible for one major article of some five thousand words, a second shorter article of some two to three thousand words, and often a third brief article on breaking news. With the help of three assistant editors and a stable of researchers, my job was to think up the story ideas, assign them to appropriate writers (both staff writers and outside writers), then edit the articles when they came in, illustrate them with pictures or drawings, and oversee their final publication.

Since high school days I have loved good writing and good writers. In this job I had total independence to go after both. In the course of six years, first as an assistant editor and then as the top editor, I dealt with several hundred different writers, some good, some bad, some wonderful. And some who were very famous.

Herewith Winston Churchill, Ernest Hemingway and Norman Mailer.

WINSTON CHURCHILL

I had the delightful task of excerpting for LIFE all four volumes of Churchill's *History of the English-Speaking Peoples*. The only bad thing about this underappreciated work is its title. Churchill wrote most of it before World War II when he was out of power, in disgrace politically, and able to devote full time to his writing. *English-Speaking Peoples* is far better written than his famous six-volume history of World War II. LIFE had excerpted that work, too, before I arrived in the Articles Department. I bought all six volumes from Book-of-the-Month but found them hard to read, full of endless memos and tiresome documents. Although I know that his account of World War II is invaluable as an historic document, I confess that I have never finished reading it, and almost certainly never will.

For an account of what it was like to negotiate with Churchill in person and to deal with his demands, see *Outsider, Insider,* the memoirs of LIFE's Publisher and Time Inc. Chairman Andrew Heiskell, who bought the magazine rights for both histories — and paid for a lot else besides, including the author's extraordinary travel and living expenses. Heiskell was a first-class businessman, but Churchill was, as you might expect, a better negotiator and a more successful demander.

My job on *English-Speaking Peoples* was to read each
long volume, decide which passages I thought were most
significant or exciting, write a short italic precede to each
passage to explain what this was about, then arrange the
passages into roughly 5,000-word segments for each issue
of the magazine. We also illustrated each segment with
lavish color photographs of the scenes described, such as
great battlefields, or with historical black-and-white
drawings or photographs, depending on what was available.

Two researchers, Jane Wilson and Caroline Zinsser,
worked with me on every excerpt from all four volumes,
more than a dozen in all, published over several years.
The three of us had a terrific time. We were working with
the words of a famous and excellent writer, and although
Jane and Caroline caught him in factual errors that had
to be corrected, it was a particular pleasure to be dealing
with such consistently marvelous words. I can't think of
a happier job for an editor than to pick and choose the
very best passages from hundreds of thousands of words
by a superb writer.

My only regret about this project is that I never got to
meet the author in person.

We were required under the contract to submit the
proposed selected passages, along with my italic precedes,
to Churchill's office in London for his approval. I was
deeply concerned, a thirty-year-old editor sending his se-
lections and his own puny words to this giant, the man
Time had recently named the Man of the Half-Century.

But I shipped my first package off to our London bureau to send to Churchill's aides who would show it to
our author. I waited with alarm.

It seemed a long time to me, but finally the London bureau sent me Churchill's answer. Everything approved as is.

I was relieved and thrilled, but now I wanted to hear more. I asked the London bureau if Churchill had said anything specific about my excerpts and precedes. They didn't know but promised to ask Churchill's aides and get back to me.

Two days later I got my answer. Churchill had indeed said something specific.

What he had said was, "Lovely, lovely."

I was even more thrilled.

But as we went on and on through all the succeeding excerpts from the succeeding volumes, everything continued to be approved. This led me to two less thrilling conclusions. First, Churchill was now in his eighties, weary from a lifetime of heavy burdens, and might not have the energy to pay close attention to LIFE's excerpts. Second, we had already paid him in full for our magazine rights, so perhaps, with all that money in his pocket, he didn't give a damn.

Perhaps. But of course I prefer to believe that he meant it when he said, "Lovely, lovely." One of my favorite quotes from a man who had many famous quotes.

ERNEST HEMINGWAY

The most influential American writer of the twentieth cen-
tury contributed two major works to LIFE. The first was
a tremendous triumph, the second a massive failure.
Lucky me, I got to edit the second. I'd always admired
him as a writer, though not as a person. After my experience I had good reason to deplore him in both categories.

The triumph was a publishing breakthrough. On
September 1, 1952, in a single issue, LIFE published the
entire text of Hemingway's new novel, *The Old Man and
the Sea*. Many magazines besides LIFE bought first serial
rights to forthcoming books. This entitled us to publish
excerpts before the books reached the bookstores. This
was big business, occupying the time and dollars of many
editors, book publishers, authors and literary agents. But
the magazines customarily bought only excerpts. Whole
books couldn't fit easily into magazines. Also book publishers considered first serial rights in magazines a come-
on for the book itself. If the whole book were published
in a magazine, even if that were physically possible, it
would destroy bookstore sales.

There were occasional exceptions, most notably in the
New Yorker, which once devoted a whole issue to John
Hersey's *Hiroshima* (a very short book) and in later years
ran all of Truman Capote's *In Cold Blood* over several

issues. But to publish an important new novel by a major writer in a single issue of a magazine with the huge circulation of LIFE was a giant publishing risk — not for LIFE but for Hemingway and his publisher. Millions of people could read the whole novel practically for free. Why, then, would they bother to buy the book?

The convoluted thinking ran as follows. Hemingway is the greatest living American novelist. (Forget about Faulkner, he doesn't sell.) This is a terrific book. Every serious reader has to have the actual book in his library, even if he read it first in LIFE. And many readers will prefer to read it as a real book, not in the floppy pages of a magazine. And LIFE's circulation, in spite of its size, is still only a small fraction of the whole population. And, as a financial safety factor, LIFE is paying a bundle.

All this speculation turned out to be true. Everybody loved *The Old Man and the Sea,* in spite of, or perhaps because of, its sentimentality. LIFE got the attention and respect and the newsstand sales that it wanted. Both the Book-of-the-Month and the nation's bookstores went on to sell buckets of copies. Hemingway and his publisher made buckets of money. Everybody was happy — except one person.

Alfred Eisenstaedt was the photographer assigned to fly down to Cuba and photograph Hemingway for the cover and for other illustration. For the rest of his life, from 1952 until his death, whenever he was asked who was his most difficult subject, Eisie answered, without a pause for thought, "Hemingway." For openers he was instructed to address Hemingway as "Papa," his famous nickname, which Eisie dutifully did. Hemingway, a lifelong anti-Semite as you can tell from the first page of his first novel, *The Sun Also Rises,* addressed Eisie as "Snake Shit." Hemingway constantly insulted and diminished him and, once in drunken anger, grabbed Eisie by his shirt and threatened to throw him off a balcony.

Papa was Eisie's least favorite LIFE cover.

I don't remember who, eight years later, made the deal for Hemingway's l960 LIFE project, *The Dangerous Summer.* I know it wasn't me, although I was articles editor and wound up in charge of it. I expect it was Ed Thompson, the managing editor. But if I had been given the chance to make the deal, I certainly would have. Hemingway was still a huge if somewhat fading name, and now he was returning to one of the subjects for which he was famous: bullfighting. His early bullfighting book, *Death in the Afternoon,* had been a success, and was still considered by many aficionados to be the definitive popular work on the subject. Now, in the summer of 1959, Hemingway proposed to cover the summer-long duel between Spain's two greatest matadors, the older master Luis Miguel Dominguin and the younger hotshot Antonio Ordonez. The Super Bowl of bullfighting reported in first person by Ernest Hemingway! He didn't know how much he would wind up writing, but we could run three long installments. Who could resist? How could it fail?

It is time to introduce A.E. Hotchner, universally known as Hotch. Professionally he was a writer of many articles and books, but his greatest talent was to be a close, trusted friend of two very famous men, Ernest Hemingway and, much later, Paul Newman. Hotch and Newman were colleagues in the Newman's Own enterprise, the successful series of Newman's quality foods, with all of the profits going to charity. Hotch's best-known book is *Papa Hemingway*, a personal memoir of his close fourteen-year friendship with the author. He was never Hemingway's agent, but because he was such a trusted friend, he often handled Hemingway's problems, of which there were more and more as Papa grew older and more irascible.

Poor Hotch. His task was to deal with LIFE as Papa's representative on *Dangerous Summer*. He also helped Papa on the selection and editing of the excerpts for LIFE. And poor Ralph. My task was to edit *Dangerous Summer* for the magazine. Both tasks proved, in the end, hopeless.

Leaving Hemingway out of it, just for a moment, the central human story of *Dangerous Summer* was superb. It is the age-old story of the brash young rising star competing with and defeating and thereby destroying the older star. An old story, but set in a different venue with vivid principal characters.

That, indeed, was Hemingway's own theme, as he followed the duel from bullring to bullring across Spain during that summer of 1959. But in the actual writing, he surrounded and embellished and finally buried his theme under oceans of bullfighting technicalities and extraneous sidebar travel stuff.

The manuscript that arrived on my desk was (I am indebted to Hotch for this number) 108,746 words long. It read even longer than that. Ed Thompson, the managing editor and only other reader, was as appalled as I was. But by this time I was an experienced and confident and, in my own opinion, outstanding editor. Within this forest of verbiage I found some fine passages, some good passages and other acceptable passages. I cut them out, had them typed up and submitted them to Thompson for a three-part publication. With minor suggestions and changes, Ed not only accepted but applauded. We had a fighting chance to escape disaster. The excerpts didn't read nearly as bad as the book. Nothing for LIFE to be ashamed of — well, not too much anyway.

So we sent the excerpts off to Hemingway and Hotch in Cuba. No dice. The telephone word came back from Hotch that Hemingway thought crucial, vital passages had, in our ignorance, been omitted. Papa would proceed to restore them.

This went back and forth for some weeks, Thompson and I trying to eliminate passages, Hemingway determined to preserve them, Hotch caught in the middle. During all this painful period I talked only to Hotch, never to Hemingway. Except once at the very end. During some kind of electrical storm, Hemingway himself got on the phone to Thompson and me. We couldn't hear him, and he couldn't hear us, despite all the shouting back and forth. So I can't report what he said, but I'm sure it was violent.

In the end, eight years to the week after the triumphant publication of *The Old Man and the Sea,* we published the first of three installments of *The Dangerous Summer.* No applause this time. And if you think this is just my misjudgment of a great writer's work, it would not be until 1985, a quarter-century after Hemingway's suicide, that a shortened version of *The Dangerous Summer* was finally published as a book. The adverse criticism was universal.

NORMAN MAILER

Three months after I got the job I had worked twenty-one years to achieve, Norman Mailer almost forced me to resign.

Mailer had never written for LIFE before. Again, as with Hemingway, I did not make the assignment, but this time, unlike Hemingway, I knew exactly how the deal was made. In 1969 Tom Griffith met Mailer at some social function and asked him if he would like to cover the moon landing for LIFE. Griffith, a highly respected *Time* editor, had the right to make this offer because he had just been named editor of LIFE. At the same time I had just been named LIFE's managing editor.

This takes a word of explanation about Time Inc. abnormalities. In most of journalism the editor is the boss and the managing editor is his deputy for operations and administration. Not at Time Inc. On all our magazines the managing editor runs the show. He controls the staff, he controls the day-to-day editorial operation, he makes the decisions on stories and covers. The editor, when and if there is one, is a more honorific position awarded to someone who has served the company well, is still held in esteem but is not old enough to retire. It is a bit of a make-work job, not really necessary, especially in the eyes of

the managing editor who has this ill-defined figure loom-
ing over his shoulder.

So Editor Tom Griffith signed up Norman Mailer to
cover the moon landing, having cleared the assignment
with Editor-in-Chief Hedley Donovan and informing me.

Again, as with Hemingway, I applauded. Mailer was
a big name, a brilliant reporter and a vivid writer, even
though he sometimes fell on his face through his own
excesses. Nothing that good editing couldn't fix.

As for the moon landing, LIFE had bought at great expense the personal stories of the astronauts. For the past
ten years we had been treading water, running dull stories
about their training and their wives. As more astronauts
were added to the program, LIFE had to add more money.
But at last Alan Shepherd flew into space and told us his
story, and John Glenn flew into orbit and told us his even
better story. And now the moon landing would be the
grand payoff for all that waiting and expense. We would of
course run the personal accounts of the three moon astronauts, but Mailer would give us his uninhibited report on
the great event, which would then become a book to be
published by Little, Brown, a company we owned.

Tom Griffith made one mistake in his deal with
Mailer. He promised that there would be no cuts in
Mailer's copy without Mailer's consent. A total promise.

The scene shifts to Houston, the NASA headquarters and
command center for all space flights. (As in, "Houston,
we have a problem," during the much later flight of
Apollo 13.) Prior to the moon launch, LIFE is giving a
huge self-promotional dinner party. I am back in New

York editing the magazine, but the banquet hall is filled with miscellaneous brass: NASA executives, astronauts, LIFE business executives, CEOs of major LIFE advertisers and, as extra window dressing, a few celebrities. Among the last is Connie Ryan, author of the famous D-Day book *The Longest Day*. He is seated at the same table with Norman Mailer, who is there both as a celebrity and as a working reporter for our story. Mailer, ever the adventurer, had recently run for New York City mayor and been resoundingly defeated in the primary. He had never expected to win, but neither had he expected such a humiliating defeat.

The master of ceremonies for this profligate evening is LIFE Publisher Jerry Hardy. A big-nosed fellow with a raucous sense of humor, he is popular with the editorial staff, including me. At the microphone before a prominent audience of bigwigs and fat cats, he is in his element. With enthusiasm and wit he introduces prominent guests, going from table to table, seating chart in front of him, asking people to stand up as he names them. When he reaches the Ryan-Mailer table. he says, "Cornelius Ryan, author of *The Longest Day,* and Norman Mailer, author of the shortest campaign." Wild laughter throughout the hall at Mailer's expense as the two writers get to their feet, one with smiling pleasure, one not.

Mailer, standing there embarrassed and blushing, says to himself, "I'll get you for this."

When it comes to holding grudges, Mailer is a champion. He leaves Houston holding a firm grudge not only against Jerry Hardy personally but against that whole LIFE banquet.

●   ●   ●

Although I had been reading Mailer ever since *The Naked and the Dead,* I never met him until he walked into my office with the first installment of his moon landing story. He was short, with bushy hair, husky, pugnacious. Not looking for a fight but available if the occasion arose. Penetrating eyes, strong handshake. Courteous. He hoped I would like the article, which he knew was too long. He said he knew LIFE aimed for five thousand word articles but he considered five thousand words a mere poker ante. He would be ready to consult after I had read it, but this was basically what he wanted us to publish.

I did read it. I did like it. But there was a problem.

He had written, with vigor and venom, about the banquet. He wrote that Jerry Hardy had the face of a clown and a flabby nose that looked like it was made out of putty. Accurate description, but not what LIFE would be eager to publish. And that was not all he wrote about the banquet. He also described the CEO of a brewing company and a major LIFE advertiser as a reeling and obnoxious drunk. Again, accurate description.

After Editor-in-Chief Hedley Donovan had read the article, he summoned me to his office. He thought it was very good and very good for LIFE, but much too long. Of course the passage describing Hardy and the banquet would have to be cut. "Yes indeed," I said, "but only if Mailer agreed." "No," Donovan said, "it had to be cut, regardless. We can't mock our own publisher and insult a major advertiser." "Yes," I said, "but Mailer has to agree." "No," Donovan said, "it has to go whether he agrees or not." I pointed out that we had made him a promise. "That doesn't matter," said Donovan, a stern, unrelenting man, "it has to go."

I went away and thought about it. I thought about it a lot. Donovan's position was understandable but, in my view, unacceptable. A promise is a promise: no cuts without Mailer's approval. It was not as though he had written scatological words, as he frequently did. That we could delete on principle. And it was not as though his banquet description could be challenged for accuracy. And he hadn't actually named either our publisher or the brewery CEO, although it would not take much detective work to figure out who they were. I would have to try to persuade him on other grounds, and his reputation for persuadability was not high. Neither, however, was Hedley Donovan's.

That night I told my wife Eleanor that I might have to resign. If Donovan insisted and Mailer also insisted, I saw no choice but to stand by Tom Griffith's promise. She was furious, though not at me. "But you just got the job!" I didn't like the idea any better than she did.

I decided that I could not mention to Mailer that my job was at stake. I refused to make any play for his sympathy, which would be demeaning to us both. Besides, it was not really the issue.

We sat face to face in my office, the marked-up manuscript between us on my desk. He knew and I knew that it was too long, so I was suggesting cuts that I wanted him to approve. And specifically, I said we wanted to cut the entire banquet description and I explained why. He heard me out, silent. When I finished, there was more silence, quite lengthy. Then he told me the story, which I was now hearing for the first time, about Jerry Hardy's longest day, shortest campaign introduction.

I was appalled and said so. "But you were there working for us."

"That's what I thought," Mailer said. Then he laughed and shrugged. "Anyway I got it off my chest. Okay, take it out. But I'll keep it in the book."

As indeed he did. You can look it up in *Of a Fire on the Moon*.

I became good friends with Norman. When we published the first installment, I put him on the cover. He was pleased, although he objected that "My face is not that pink." (He was right, poor engraving.) We worked comfortably together through the publication of all the installments of his moon landing story. He was professionally serious about his copy, working in my office until the last page had been approved by us both. I had offered him a drink but he said no thanks. As soon as the first closing was over, he said, "Now I'll have a glass of bourbon." All managing editors (and a number of other Time Inc.-ers) kept a liquor cabinet for just such occasions — and for various other occasions as well. I, a vodka man who had last drunk bourbon in college, pulled out a bottle of vodka and a bottle of Jack Daniel's. Norman shook his head at me in disgust. "That's not real bourbon." He drank it anyway, copiously but with limited relish. From then on I kept real bourbon for him in my liquor cabinet.

One of the two best articles I published during my many years at LIFE was Norman Mailer's account of the first Ali-Frazier heavyweight championship fight. (The other was an article on a cancer surgeon by W.C. Heinz.).

Heavyweight boxing has been a dismal scene for decades, but back in 1971 it was a major event. This was thanks mostly to Muhammad Ali, who gets every sport superlative I can think of: best boxer, best athlete, best talker, best looking, most exciting and all-around flashiest man. His upcoming championship fight with Joe Frazier was such a huge expectation that it made the cover of LIFE, *Time* and *Sports Illustrated* all in the same week. Hedley Donovan, himself an active follower of sports, was a bit miffed that all three of his biggest magazines chose the same cover subject in the same week. Was nothing else going on in the world? At his weekly managing editors lunch he hoped that only *Sports Illustrated* would run a cover on the actual fight. I said I couldn't promise for LIFE. "Norman Mailer is covering it for us, and if it's a good fight, it could make the cover." Hedley said he hoped not.

Norman, an expert on boxing and a special fan of Ali, had agreed to the assignment long before. A minor amateur boxer himself, like Hemingway, he was excited about covering a big fight under a fierce deadline. So was I. The fight would take place on a Monday night in Madison Square Garden and, delaying our normal closing date at considerable expense, I could give Norman until Wednesday night to write and close his story. Of course sports reporters do this all the time on an even-tighter overnight deadline, but major writers, with major reputations to defend, are never asked to write a major story so fast.

Because Norman and I had agreed on the assignment early, he had time to visit both training camps and to write a large portion of his story in advance of the fight.

His portraits of Ali and Frazier working out before the fight are brilliant.

Norman, like our photographers, had a near ringside

seat. I was there too, in a good but more distant seat. Of all the sports events I have attended over many years in many sports, this was the greatest. The stakes were high (heavyweight champion of the world), the setting was perfect (Madison Square Garden), expectation and excitement were intense, and the two opponents were supremely different in style and character, the brilliant and dashing Ali, the powerful and relentless Frazier.

The fight went fifteen rounds. Ali was knocked down for the first time in his gorgeous career. Frazier won by decision. It was a sensational, wonderful fight.

Over the next two days Norman's report arrived in my office, small sections at a time. He, at home in Brooklyn, wrote everything longhand and his assistant Judith McNeil, accustomed to his difficult handwriting, typed it up and sent it to me by messenger. Wonderful stuff, section by section by section. Judith and I talked often — I'm sending this, yes I got it — but Norman and I talked only once. He speculated in his copy that the judges and referee could have changed their votes on the earlier rounds in favor of Frazier, once he knocked Ali down, thus giving Frazier the decision he did not deserve. Norman wanted to believe that Ali won, despite the knockdown. Compared to me, he knew everything about boxing rules and I knew nothing, but I knew this one. I phoned to remind him that the judges and the referee have to hand in their votes at the end of each round. No way they can later change their round-by-round vote. He accepted this, reluctantly, and changed his copy.

We closed on time Wednesday night. On the March 19 cover I billed "Norman Mailer on the Fight" along with an action picture. Sorry, Hedley.

When the dust had settled, I told Norman what a terrific piece he had written. He cheerfully agreed. And then he said, referring back to the solid, interesting but less-than-fabulous moon landing installments for which we had paid a fortune, "I owed you one."

ONE WEEK'S DEAD

All through my LIFE years I looked at many thousands of pictures and helped pick the ones that we published. Many marvelous pictures that people still remember: tragic, beautiful, heartbreaking, hilarious, shocking, newsworthy, historical. We ran those pictures big, sometimes full page, sometimes a two-page spread. Our readers loved these great pictures.

But the most moving, most emotional story I ever worked on did not have a single great picture, not even what you could call a good picture. In fact, it had 217 tiny pictures, all the same size, none of them significant. In truth, they were individually dull.

But together, row on row over twelve pages, they broke everybody's heart, very much including my own. Of all the stories about the Vietnam War, on television or in magazines and newspapers, I think it had the greatest impact.

It was called "One Week's Dead."

I wish I could claim it was my idea, but it wasn't. What I can claim is that I was the editor who ran the story, and I ran it in the first month after I got the top job. What I have to admit is that in the remaining three years of our magazine's existence, I never again ran a story with such emotional impact. On the other hand, in my opinion, neither did my predecessors.

The idea came from an assistant managing editor named Loudon Wainwright. He had long been my best friend on the magazine, as well as a competitor for the top job, as well as one of our best writers ever. He had been struck by the fact that week after week during the Vietnam War the Pentagon kept announcing the number of Americans killed, but it was only a number. Wainwright, a deeply sensitive man, said to himself — and eventually to others — these shouldn't be just numbers. These are people. These are real people. LIFE should find a way to say that — and show that.

Loudon Wainwright and Phil Kunhardt, another close friend and assistant managing editor, worked up the idea of taking a single week out of the Vietnam War and turning the Pentagon's number of the dead into pictures of the real soldiers who died. I knew about this project and heartily endorsed it, but it wasn't my show.

It was important to choose an ordinary week of the war. We must not pick some week where a big battle inflated the casualties. It must be a plain ordinary week when an ordinary number of American soldiers had been killed. In the week that we chose, May 28 through June 3, 1969, there was no big battle, nothing the least bit special except, as Wainwright wrote in his opening textblock, it included Memorial Day.

That week's dead turned out to be 242. The Pentagon released the names and last known addresses of those dead. The rest was up to us to track them down and get their pictures.

Try to imagine what that involved. Pretend that you

are the parent or wife or brother or sister or fiancée of a man who has just been killed in Vietnam. Right now it doesn't matter whether you or your lost man was for or against this war. What matters to you is that he is dead. And now, immediately after his death, you get a phone call or a visit from some total stranger, a somebody from LIFE, explaining what the magazine plans to do and asking, please, for a picture.

All across the country LIFE correspondents and researchers and stringers made that profoundly intimate and invasive request, phone to phone or door to door. In that terrible moment of loss almost everybody said yes and gave us a picture. Sometimes they said this is my only picture, please be sure to send it back.

I am certain of two things. All those relatives believed in what LIFE was trying to do, to turn those abstract numbers into faces. And they cooperated because LIFE was still a nationally beloved magazine.

Of the 242 dead that week we got 217 pictures. Of the twenty-five we didn't get, some could not be found at the last known address. Only a minute handful of relatives said no. I have never seen such passionate concern on the part of our staff to avoid any mistakes on this story. Every picture was logged in and protected. All we planned to write under each picture was name, age, rank, branch of service and hometown. Every word and spelling was meticulously checked for accuracy.

A word on staff motivation. By June 1969 many of us were opposed to the war, but this opposition was by no means universal. Many who worked on the story still believed in the war and in eventual victory. But all of us, whether for or against the war, believed in what we were trying to do with this story, to turn those blank numbers into human faces.

When all the pictures were in and the layouts made, I had to clear our proposed story with Editor-in-Chief Hedley Donovan. This was a special hazard. Donovan was still a strong proponent of the Vietnam War. He had written major signed editorials in LIFE defending the war and urging that we pursue it to the hilt. He believed in eventual success. Would he now approve our story? Or would he tell us not to run it? I was after all a brand new-and untested top editor.

We spread out all the pages on my layout table, and Donovan came down to look at them. Wainwright and Kunhardt, the progenitors, were in the room. Donovan walked down the line, looking at the pages. An enormous amount of silence. He said nothing, we said nothing.

Then he told us, all right, run it.

When he walked out of the room, headed for the elevator back to his office, we all smiled and hugged each other, but were careful not to say anything that Hedley might hear. We had won.

Hedley wrote later in his memoir that the main reason he had approved our story was because all those bereaved people had given LIFE their pictures, and he felt that we could not disappoint them. Good for him.

I made a mistake in choosing the cover. I chose a single grainy face out of all the pictures because I thought it was haunting. I still do, looking at it today, but it gave no indication of the real story inside the magazine. If I had it to do over again, I would run a section of the actual story, some faces with their captions, so that people would understand what we were doing.

As a result of my cover choice, the issue did not sell well on the newsstands, always a key barometer of commercial success. No matter. The emotional success was overwhelming.

Even I, who had spent hours looking at the layouts, was astonished when I held the actual magazine in my hands. I turned those pages, page after page, looking at all those young faces, row after row, all the same size, just like a high school yearbook. Just like a yearbook except for the fact that every single one of them had just been killed.

The whole country cried. Not realizing what an enormous effort it had taken to produce this story, some people suggested that we do this story every week until the war ended. A couple of letter writers, thinking that LIFE could do anything, suggested we do a similar story on One Week's Dead among the Viet Cong enemy.

People thought LIFE could do anything — and sometimes we could.

LIFE's 1969 story has been repeated over and over again during the Iraq War. First and most memorably by Ted Koppel, who devoted a long TV program to showing the names and faces of all our Iraq dead, acknowledging that this grew out of LIFE's 1969 story. Since then the device has been repeated over and over on television and in newspapers.

I approve. I hope that never again, in any war, will we settle for numbers. We must see the names and the faces.

BOONDOGGLES

The mere padding of expense accounts is of little interest and worth no attention. It happens all the time in every company. Only when superior imagination or wit or skullduggery is involved should we pay any notice.

LIFE Photographer Bob Landry is famous for two things. He took the sexy picture of Rita Hayworth in a black nightgown kneeling on a bed, a candidate for the best pin-up ever. And he got caught padding his expense account with taxi fares. Everybody throws in an occasional phony taxi, but one month Landry had a flock of them. The picture editor, who had to approve all photographer expense accounts, realized that while Landry was claiming those cab fares, he had actually been shooting a story on board a U.S. Navy aircraft carrier. Challenged to explain all those taxis while he was at sea, Landry came back with this inspired explanation: "It was a very long aircraft carrier."

One hotshot young photographer named Paul Schutzer could not bring himself to fill out expense accounts. He kept drawing advances but could not be bothered to account for them. When he fell six months and thousands of dollars behind, the picture editor brought the problem to me, and we figured out an ingenious solution. Until he handed in expense accounts for all those months and dollars, he could 1) draw no more advances and 2) get no more assignments. The second proviso was devastating to Schutzer, an eager, dedicated photographer who loved to work.

Three weeks later he turned in his expense accounts for the whole six months along with many appropriate receipts. The entry on the final month's reckoning that earned him a place in legend was "Fee for preparation of expense accounts — $500." The preparer was an accountant who happened to be his father-in-law. We disallowed that item, but let Schutzer go back to work.

So much for small-time shenanigans. Now for a big-time boondoggle.

In 1961 George Hunt was named managing editor of LIFE. A tall, strikingly handsome man, he had been a decorated Marine combat officer in World War II. He promptly fired or retired half a dozen top executives who had been in place far too long and chose three new assistant M.E.s, including me. We were all younger and less experienced than our new boss. George Hunt was a highly creative man with a vivid imagination and the readiness of a combat U.S Marine to charge any position or capture any hill. After two years in power he came up with a stupendous idea. He called his three A.M.E.s into his office for a conference and told us to close the doors.

The three of us were, he said, too inexperienced to be the top editors of the world's most important magazine. We did not know enough about the great world outside America, about world art, about world culture, about world leaders. How could we come up with great story suggestions if we didn't know the wide world we lived in? He was going to fix that, beginning this year, beginning right now. He had decided that every year each of us would take a one-month tour, to any place in the world of our choice, at company expense. This would be in addition to our regular month of vacation. This tour must not be thought of as extra vacation, this was a working trip, and we would be expected to behave accordingly. No lying around on beaches. We must plan our trips carefully in consultation with bureaus and stringers, we must interview important figures.

We looked at George. We looked at each other. Could he possibly be serious?

Yes, he was serious, and it was about to get even better.

Such a tour, away from home for a whole month, would be a terrible emotional hardship for our wives. Therefore, George said, we could take our wives with us — also at full company expense. There were only two rules. Rule One: the three of us could not go to the same country or same area in the same year. Rule Two: only one of us could be away on this tour at any given time because he needed at least two of us on hand to help him run the magazine.

We thought we could endure these restrictions!

I can't remember how soon we learned that George Hunt and his wife, Anita, would also participate in this fantastic boondoggle. They, too, would explore the world for one month a year at company expense.

During the next five years my wife Eleanor and I took the following free-ride tours: 1) western Europe; 2) east Asia, including Australia, the Philippines, Japan; 3) the entire Middle East; 4) a private African safari; 5) eastern

Europe, including Russia. My two A.M.E. colleagues had similar jaunts with their wives. So did George Hunt with his wife. All of this was first class, no coach flights, no second-rate hotels.

I recall only one direct overlap with my fellow travelers, but it was memorable.

My wife and I arrived in mid-afternoon at the lofty and elegant Istanbul Hilton, where the manager himself welcomed us effusively. He was so happy to have another distinguished LIFE couple, just like Mr. and Mrs. Hunt a year ago.

Half an hour later, while we were still unpacking in what we considered too splendid a suite, the doorbell rang.

It was the smiling manager again, followed by a waiter pushing a cart. On the cart were a bucket of iced champagne with two properly chilled flutes and a large container of Beluga caviar, nestled in crushed ice and accompanied by plates, silverware, toast points, sliced egg whites and lemon wedges. For several years we had been enjoying first-class accommodations on these free tours, but this was at last too much for LIFE to have to pay for.

"I'm sorry, I didn't order this," I told the manager. "We don't want this."

He looked pained. "But it's what Mr. and Mrs. Hunt ordered."

Of course we all enlarged our knowledge of the world. Of course we all came back with ideas for stories, some of which eventually appeared in the magazine. I wrote three published articles based on my trips, and my colleagues also wrote occasional pieces. I'm sure that George Hunt thought his extravagant idea had paid off for the magazine.

I very much doubt it. What it mainly accomplished was to give all of us, and all our wives, a marvelous time, absolutely free.

George Hunt was the best boss I ever had. During his eight years as M.E. I sat in the office right next to him. He was an exciting and brilliant leader. No editor was ever more sincere, more honorable. He was never devious in any way. He *believed* in those tours. But I suspect that, like other Marines, he was probably convinced that whatever he had decided to do must surely be right.

GUESS WHO ELECTED JFK

In Rick Perlstein's 2008 book *Nixonland*, he names the people Richard Nixon blamed for his bitterly narrow loss of the 1960 presidential election to John Kennedy. On page fifty he writes, "Henry Luce, the imperious publisher of *Life,* getting cold feet and pulling at the last minute an article by Billy Graham that was to urge the evangelist's millions of devoted acolytes not to vote for a man just because he was 'more handsome and more charming.' " And then he cites Nixon again on page fifty-nine: "Of all the explanations for the margin between victory and defeat in 1960, his favorite was Henry Luce's withdrawing the Billy Graham article."

Nixon's view is of course extreme. Just for instance, what about that crucial first Nixon-Kennedy TV debate, where Kennedy killed him? What about all the other issues during that campaign? But we all know that Nixon always found somebody else to blame for whatever went wrong. This time, however, he blamed the wrong person. It wasn't Henry Luce, it was the articles editor of *Life,* who happened to be me. When I read Perlstein's book, I learned, forty-eight years after the event, that I was responsible for his defeat — although he thought it was Luce, not me.

Henry Luce did not get cold feet about that Billy

Graham article. The man who started *Fortune* during the Great Depression, the man who kept publishing *Sports Illustrated* through a decade of large losses until it finally became a success, did not suffer from cold feet syndrome. He was, however, highly opinionated and often unfair on three major subjects: China, the Republican Party and Christianity. The Billy Graham puffy endorsement of Nixon represented two out of those three. Luce thought it was important publishable news that a prominent southern evangelist was gung ho for Nixon.

I did not. As articles editor, I thought it would be unfair and improper to publish such a piece unless we gave equal time and space to some major public figure who, equally surprisingly, endorsed Kennedy. LIFE had an editorial page where Luce could say whatever he wanted to, often to the dismay of the staff, especially during election years. Because *Time* had no such escape hatch, Luce's political preferences far more frequently made their way into *Time*'s "news" stories. I believed that the existence of Luce's editorial page in LIFE should protect us against that.

Fortunately LIFE's Managing Editor Ed Thompson supported my position on the Graham article. If he hadn't, the Graham article would have run over my protest. Luce was unhappy about Thompson's and my stand, but he urged us to find a matching author who supported Kennedy, and then we could run both articles. We did not find a similar Kennedy supporter, so we did not publish Billy Graham. Luce was annoyed and frustrated but no cold feet were involved. Nixon just did not know what had really happened.

Although perhaps he should have. I was the editor

who later handled the LIFE excerpts form Nixon's autobiographical book *Six Crises*. I flew out to Los Angeles
to consult with Nixon about the project. I arrived at the
handsome house in suburban Bel Air that some wealthy
supporter had lent to the Nixons. The front door was
open. I knocked on the screen door and was instantly answered by furious barking. Yes, it was Checkers himself,
the hero of Nixon's famous "Checkers Speech" that had
insured his nomination as Eisenhower's vice president.
Checkers knew instinctively that I was dangerous, even
if his master did not.

When I first came to LIFE as a young researcher straight
out of college, I was trained in the severe Time Inc. checking system. Never take any statement for granted, even if
it looks true. Check every name, every fact, every number,
every source.

Well, not this time. I am not going to check with
Nixonland author Rick Perlstein about his statements in
the Billy Graham matter. I am not going to check the
sources he cites in his notes. I am not going to check the
Time Inc. Archives for anything Luce himself may have
said on this subject.

If you are offered a footnote in history, even an anony-
mous footnote, take it. As far as I am concerned, Nixon
was dead right. Because I blocked the Billy Graham article, I cost him the 1960 election. Even if Nixon didn't
know it. Even if only Checkers and I knew it.

TEDDY WHITE AND CAMELOT

Theodore H. White, one of America's best political reporters, wrote a series of original and successful books called *The Making of the President*. The first came in 1960, the story of the Kennedy-Nixon campaign and election, which we excerpted in LIFE. It was followed every four years by another account of another campaign and election, also excerpted in LIFE.

I had barely heard of Teddy White when David Maness, an editor in my Articles Department, suggested that we assign him to cover an important political story. Maness and White had known each other well at *Collier's*, a recently defunct general magazine. (They all died eventually: first *Collier's*, then *Saturday Evening Post*, then *Look* and last of all LIFE.) Maness vouched for White as a first-class, reliable writer, and I agreed to sign him up.

An older colleague who had worked on *Time* heard about this assignment and asked me if I had cleared it with Luce. I said I didn't have to clear assignments with Luce. Well, he said, you better clear this one. And he told me the story.

Teddy White, as a young man, had been Luce's favorite *Time* correspondent. Stationed in China, he reported stories that interested Luce more than any other subject. When Luce visited China, or when White came back to New York on home leave, they discussed China endlessly and with intense enthusiasm.

But then White's reporting took a turn that Luce, and therefore *Time,* could not stomach. White reported the corruption and weakness of Nationalist China under its ruler Chiang Kai-shek and his wife, Madame Chiang Kai-shek. To Luce these were sainted figures. He knew them personally, they were his friends, and China was his birthplace. Furthermore White saw and reported that the Communists and Mao Tse-Tung were gaining now and would win in the end. This was too much. White's reporting was changed by *Time* editors. The situation became impossibly bitter and, said my older colleague, "Teddy either quit or was fired — take your pick." White and Luce had not spoken for years.

After hearing this background, I indeed thought I'd better clear the assignment with Luce. He might well order me to cancel it. I thought I'd better do it in person, not over the phone or by memo, so I told his secretary I needed to see him — briefly. I had no idea how brief it was going to be.

Luce was reading at his desk when I walked in. He looked up.

"Harry," I said, "LIFE's made an assignment that I think you ought to know about. We've asked Teddy White to do a piece for us."

The big bushy eyebrows shot up. "Oh?" It took him only a few seconds to absorb this bombshell. Then he said, "Good!" and went back to his reading.

When I reported Luce's reaction to Teddy, he was delighted. Peace in our time!

• • •

Teddy White was a short, gnomish figure, very Jewish, energetic, a quick sense of humor and a quick laugh for other people's wit. After that first okay from Luce, he did many articles for us, always working with his old friend Dave Maness. Together they figured out a price scale. For long, complicated articles involving lengthy research and interviewing, Teddy got our top fee. But for a short, quick piece, what Teddy and Dave christened a "White Fang" piece, meaning in and out quickly like Jack London's great fighting dog, Teddy got $1,500.

His most famous article, one of the most famous and influential short articles ever published, was a White Fang.

When Kennedy was assassinated in Dallas by Lee Harvey Oswald on November 23, 1963, the entire world of journalism focused all week long on this stupendous event. Television, radio, newspapers, magazines, it was a total commitment to telling this story. LIFE did its part by buying and publishing the Abe Zapruder film, the only frame-by-frame film record of the assassination, which would become endless evidence for the investigating Warren Commission and for every assassination theorist for years to come. In that first week Teddy White wrote a moving short article about Kennedy's body arriving back in Washington.

All that week, as everybody who was alive during those days remembers, the country watched television, entranced by this extraordinary moment of history. Oswald was murdered by Jack Ruby, on live television. Just before Kennedy's body was carried up the steps of the

Capitol to lie in state, that bouncy martial tune "Hail to the Chief" was played in mournful slow time, an emotional shock to those who were listening. That gorgeous funeral procession with the Kennedys, all in black, leading the way, Jackie in a thin black veil so we could all see her face, followed by numerous heads of state, including, most memorably for me, the lofty Charles De Gaulle and the diminutive Emperor Haile Selassie. And, of course, the tiny figure of Kennedy's son John-John saluting his father's coffin.

Jackie Kennedy was the visual heroine of this monumental event, and also the planner and arranger for much of what happened. (She told John-John when he could "salute your father.") After it was all over, she retreated to the Kennedy compound in Hyannisport, but she was not quite finished. She still had something important that she wanted to say. Because Teddy White was a famous reporter, and a good Kennedy friend, and had written that wonderful pro-Kennedy book *Making of the President 1960,* and had just written that LIFE piece about her husband's body arriving back in Washington, and finally — this is a great big finally — whatever he wrote would appear in LIFE, she decided to say what she had to say to Teddy White. So on November 29, six days after the assassination, she put in a phone call to him.

Jackie wanted to say something important that had not yet been said. Would Teddy be willing to come up to Hyannisport and listen to her and then write it for LIFE?

Yes, of course.

Good. Right now, tonight, for next week's issue?

With the possible exception of Franklin and Eleanor

Roosevelt, no White House family appreciated and used the press more than the Kennedys.

Both Jackie and Teddy knew the magazine was closing tonight. Teddy told Jackie he would have to check with the editors. He called Maness and filled him in. Maness called me because I was sitting in for Managing Editor George Hunt, who was away. We agreed to leave two pages open and hold the magazine for whatever Jackie wanted to say.

Unfortunately, the northeast was suffering a heavy rainstorm. No chance for Teddy to fly, so he hired a car and was driven through the rain to Hyannisport.

Maness and I and a skilled copyroom typist waited to hear from him. We waited and waited. The rest of the magazine had closed. I had a one-spread story laid out, written and closed as a substitute in case Jackie and Teddy didn't produce anything.

Close to midnight Teddy called in. He sounded very tired. He slowly dictated the story he had written after his long talk with Jackie.. We assumed that Jackie was right beside him, possibly on another phone, listening to every word, but during the next hour we never heard her voice.

What Teddy read us was only a short article, but it invented and nailed down the Kennedy legend of Camelot. The article was written in the third person, and Teddy never used her name. It was just "She remembers . . ." As Jackie told it, Jack Kennedy loved the Broadway musical *Camelot* about King Arthur's court. She said that at night when they were alone in their White House bedroom, he used to play the *Camelot* album, and the song he loved best was the last one:

Don't let it be forgot
That once there was a spot
For one brief shining moment
That was known as Camelot.

In this brief article she mentioned *Camelot* three times. There were other things.

She told how, just before the fatal shots, riding in that open car in her pink suit in the Texas heat, she had looked ahead to the underpass and thought how she would be cool in just a few moments. She told how in the Dallas hospital when Jack was pronounced dead, she asked to go into the surgical room alone so that she could say good-bye to him. His body was naked on the table. She stroked his feet.

Maness and I were deeply moved by the entire article, and we told Teddy so, knowing that Jackie herself must be right there to hear our sincere compliments.

Teddy then said, "We are all friends of the Kennedy family." (Indeed we were, that week the whole country was.) "Is there anything you think should be changed."

I had made a few notes to myself while Teddy was reading. I said, "Yes, just two things. I think it's too intimate, too private, about stroking his feet. I suggest cutting that. And there are too many mentions of *Camelot*. I think you should take out the last one."

"Just a minute." The phone was quiet for several minutes while he and Jackie consulted. Then Teddy came back on. "Yes, take out the sentence about the feet. But *Camelot*, that stays."

It stayed forever.

We ran the story on the final spread of the issue, no

pictures, a broad, pale gray border around the whole spread, with the headline: "For President Kennedy: An Epilogue."

Our lawyer, who read all copy to protect us against any legal problems, told me I had to run a copyright notice on the *Camelot* song at the bottom of the spread. I refused. I did not want anything to mar the severe simplicity and dignity of those pages. I promised to take care of it some other way.

Next morning I called Alan Jay Lerner, who wrote the song. I had recently met him at some party. I told him about the story and the song and why I couldn't run the copyright. We would deal with it in the Letters column in the following issue. Lerner was totally understanding.

At the time of publication everybody was convinced the story was not only wonderful but word-for-word true. Later, when the profound emotions of that event had died down, I began to doubt the details. So did other journalists who knew the Kennedys better than I did. We all thought that *Camelot* was far more likely Jackie's invention, rather than her husband's devotion to the song. Teddy White was one of the journalists who thought this.

Many years later when he and I were talking about the incredible impact of that little story, Teddy said, with a laugh, that it could have had even more impact. He asked if I remembered asking him over the phone that night to delete the sentence about Jackie stroking his feet. Yes, I remembered. Teddy said, "She told me she fondled his prick."

ZEPPELIN PILOTS

I really hated moving to the thirty-fourth floor, the corporate headquarters of Time Inc. I was happy right where I was. I was one of three assistant managing editors of LIFE, and we were competing to become the next managing editor. I liked my chances, I had a lot of responsibility and authority, and I loved what I was doing.

Instead, I was hauled away to the thirty-fourth floor to become the deputy of Editor-in-Chief Hedley Donovan. An appalling and meaningless title came with this job: senior staff editor. Nobody could figure out what that was supposed to mean. My predecessor, Tom Griffith, gave me some advice. He said that Hedley Donovan would not necessarily tell me what to do, so I would have to create my own activities. He told me that he had decided to become the best-informed editor in Time Inc. by reading every important publication. With some pride he gave me his reading list. It contained forty newspapers and magazines from all over the world. I had zero interest in his reading list. I would have to find something else to do.

I can see now that it was a huge compliment for Donovan to pick me as his deputy out of all the assistant M.E.s on all our magazines. He was getting a closer look at me, and eventually he did pick me to be the next M.E. of LIFE. But at the time I did not feel complimented, I felt screwed.

A large part of my problem was the thirty-fourth floor itself. For years I had been used to crammed offices, lots of people, lots of action, bustling corridors. On the corporate floor the thickly carpeted corridors were three times as wide, but there was nobody in them. The main inhabitants of the corridors were tall, artificial potted trees. Gary Valk, a magazine activist like me, was once exiled to thirty-four. When asked what he did, he said, "I mow the carpets."

Stepping out of the elevator on thirty-four, you met a large but spectacularly uninviting reception area. Two secretaries sat behind a long desk with banks of telephones. They made sure that no improper visitors got into this sacred precinct. Facing them were several small couches that were dominated by towering cylindrical bookcases containing bound volumes of all our magazines. I never saw anybody consult any of those volumes.

It was a very quiet floor. The offices were far more spacious than on the magazine working floors, and they were self-decorated at the whim of the occupant. The treasurer, for instance, had installed antique furniture. Most people on the floor had secretaries, whose offices would be considered quite grand at LIFE for a writer or even for the editor of a small department. Of course these were all window offices. On the inner, non-window part of the floor was a vast conference room, big enough to contain a small zeppelin. It was rarely used for conferences or anything else.

This silent, sumptuous floor was occupied in good part by extremely important people. These included the editor-in-chief, the chairman, the president, the treasurer, the magazine director, the personnel director. But I thought a number of people on thirty-four did not seem important at all. Why were they here?

I made friends with a kindred spirit named Bernie Yudain, who had a cheerful sense of humor and was a fellow-sufferer in the stodgy thirty-fourth floor atmosphere. He too had been dragged away from a job he loved as a corporate ambassador in Washington, D.C. to become an assistant to the president and the director of public affairs, a new job that was no better defined than senior staff editor. I asked him what all these other people did.

Bernie said, "They don't do anything. They're zeppelin pilots."

When I looked puzzled, he explained.

"Nobody flies zeppelins anymore, right? But that's the only thing these folks know how to do. They are trained to fly zeppelins, but that's it. So they still come down to the hangar every morning, and they just sit around waiting for something good to happen."

Bernie told me that when he became a thirty-fourth floor zeppelin pilot, an ad salesman friend who was a former navy pilot sent him a traditional white silk scarf.

I felt that I, too, was a zeppelin pilot. I had this big office and this silly title, but my duties were mysterious. Hedley Donovan, as Tom Griffith had predicted, did not give me many specific assignments. He told me to "supervise" *Time* and *Sports Illustrated,* but how I supervised them was left to me to figure out. The two M.E.s,

Otto Fuerbringer at *Time* and Andre Laguerre at *SI*, were longtime powerhouse bosses in charge of successful magazines. While they reported to and served at the pleasure of the editor-in-chief, they certainly did not view the relatively young and relatively inexperienced senior staff editor in that light. Otto Fuerbringer, who had a well-earned reputation for dictatorship, was surprisingly gracious to me and actually listened to my points and discussed them with me. Although I knew a lot about sports, Laguerre could barely conceal his contempt for my role and my comments. I learned something from both of them, but the impact of my supervision was minimal.

I was used to late hours at LIFE. On closing night for each issue a lot of us were there until two or three in the morning. In contrast, the thirty-fourth floor was deserted at five thirty, all those zeppelin pilots catching their trains home to the suburbs.

One night I stayed late writing a memo. No sound anywhere. I was alone.

Suddenly I did hear a sound. It was a sharp, repetitive *whish! — whish! — whish!* I was not alone after all. Something was steadily approaching down the corridor toward my office. It was a threatening sound, like a Hollywood horror movie when some unseen Terrible Creature is heard approaching a closed door. You don't know what it is, you just hear it. Nearer, nearer — *whish! — whish!*

I was actually alarmed, but at last I got up to see what it was.

It was the cleaning woman with a feather duster. She was rhythmically brushing off the leaves of the potted trees.

This was the most exciting thing that happened during my career as senior staff editor. In later years I returned to the thirty-fourth floor in two other guises, as corporate editor and as editorial director. My titles were better, but the floor stayed the same.

TWO-AND-A-HALF GIANTS

The cliché runs like this:

Citizen: "Oh, you're a journalist. You must meet such interesting people."

Journalist: "Yes, and most of them are journalists."

Only the most self-important journalist could have dreamed that up. Yes, we journalists do meet a lot of interesting people, and yes, some of them are fellow journalists. But the most interesting are not.

During my long years in journalism, the three most interesting people I knew came from other fields. Two were giants in their fields, and the third was a former almost giant. A special bonus was that I spent time with each of them over a number of years.

MARIA CALLAS

As LIFE's Chicago bureau chief, I assigned myself the Maria Callas story. I did not like opera, and I had never heard Callas sing, not even on recordings. In fact, I had never seen an opera. Growing up on Bing Crosby, Artie Shaw and Glenn Miller, I had no use for classical music of any kind. But I did know a good story when one fell in front of me, and Callas was a good story.

In 1954, the moment of her approaching American debut in Chicago, she was the most famous opera singer in the world — and also the most difficult and temperamental and demanding. Everywhere she sang, in great opera houses all over the world except in her native country, she made trouble and headlines along with the rave reviews. Just for instance, she had perversely chosen the obscure Lyric Opera in Chicago for her American debut instead of the Metropolitan Opera in New York. Everybody who was good enough debuted at the Met, but not Callas. The Lyric was reopening after years of shutdown, and she had elected to be the grand reopener. It was not lost on anybody, certainly not on Callas, that here she would be the whole show.

She had chosen to sing *Norma, La Traviata* and *Lucia di Lammermoor* in that order. Okay with me. I didn't know anything about any of them, but that would not be the point of LIFE's story. The point would be Callas herself.

Along with myself, I assigned our best bureau photographer John Dominis. When we reported for duty to Carol Fox, the director of the Lyric, she gave us strict marching orders. She was of course glad that LIFE was covering this fantastic musical event, but she knew how LIFE photographers worked. There was to be absolutely none of that. We were not to badger Callas. We must not make special requests or ask her to do anything just for the camera. We must not interrupt or interfere in any way. Yes, we could shoot the dress rehearsal of *Norma* but only from an orchestra seat and with no flash. And don't move and don't talk while Callas is rehearsing. She is very strict about rehearsals.

So Dominis and I sat side by side in row A orchestra seats in an empty auditorium, facing the empty stage across the orchestra pit.

Callas came out dressed all in white with a long flowing cape. I learned later that she was supposed to be a Druid priestess. Okay by me. The only thing I cared about was the pictures Dominis would get.

She was perhaps five feet six, long dark hair, dramatically slim, unlike in days gone by when she had been as hefty as the heftiest Wagnerian soprano. Her face was not beautiful but arresting: huge eyes, strong nose, a narrow face with strong lines. As soon as she walked out, one could feel — I know no other word for it — a presence, a commanding presence. It was only a rehearsal, but she *owned* that stage.

During this portion of the rehearsal I loved the way she handled that white cape. While singing, while moving, she swirled and trailed the cape behind her and around her. Good pictures.

When the scene was finished and everybody took a break, Dominis said, "I can't get pictures from here. I'm too far away."

No pictures, no story. "What do you want to do?"

"I could shoot better from the wings. Ask her."

Ho-ho. I was not about to ask a favor of the terrible Maria Callas. I found Carol Fox, explained the problem and asked if she would ask Callas to let Dominis shoot from the wings instead.

"Not me," said Carol Fox. "I don't want any trouble with her. You'll have to ask her yourself. But don't upset her! Don't make her angry!"

Well, again, no pictures, no story. I went backstage and found Callas just outside her dressing room, still dressed in her white Druid costume with the long cape. She knew LIFE was covering her debut, but we hadn't met.

I said I was the LIFE reporter, and we shook hands. During the eighteen years that I knew Maria Callas, we always shook hands, hello and goodbye. Never even a peck on the cheek. Although we worked together on stories and came to like and to trust each other, it was always professional.

Standing right in front of her, I was struck by her huge, brilliant eyes. They looked straight at me with total concentration while I explained the problem. The photographer and I loved the way she moved that cape, I said, and we wanted to get good action pictures. But we couldn't do it from those orchestra seats. Too far away, not enough light. Would it be possible — would she consider — letting him shoot from the corner of the stage?

When I had finished my plea, Callas said, "You should see the cape I use in *Medea*. It's dark red, and it's longer and heavier. You have to control it entirely with your wrists. Yes, your photographer can be closer. He can even shoot on stage. It won't bother me."

This was my first encounter with the most difficult singer in opera.

Her decision was, of course, not just generosity. A big story in LIFE is worth a mass, so if the photographer needed better pictures, she would help him get them. I later learned two things about Callas that, perhaps, bore on her decision, both for and against. Against her decision was the fact that she considered rehearsals essential and sacred. All through her career she demanded lengthy rehearsal time, seeking for perfection, and she despised all the people — conductors, tenors, mezzo-sopranos — who were unwilling to rehearse as hard and as long as she wanted to. So why let a photographer on stage? But in favor of her decision was the fact that she was near-sighted, and because contact lenses irritated her eyes, she could not wear them and was always sort of half-blind on stage. So Dominis being on stage during rehearsal might, indeed, not bother her because she probably didn't see him.

Whatever her reason or motivation, Dominis was right on stage beside her, kneeling down, shooting picture after picture as she twirled her white cape (controlled by her wrists). John was excited about his pictures.

On debut night the auditorium was of course sold out, and Callas got her usual rave reviews next day for her performance of *Norma*, her signature operatic role. John shot performance pictures, backstage pictures, dressing room pictures. The evening was a great success for Callas, for the Lyric and for Chicago.

But, alas, not for LIFE.

The magazine's story was, for me, a disaster and an embarrassment. It was only two back-to-back pages. The opening page was a picture of the audience, and the headline was "Opera Is Grand Again in Chicago" — as if that were the story. The second page had two small pictures of Callas in her white costume — from the waist up, no cape. After all that special cooperation from Callas, that was all we got, and all she got. But if she complained, as she had every right to, she did not complain to me. I spoke to her at a reception after the story came out, and though she talked to me, she made no comment.

I had not enjoyed *Norma* (I have to admit I still don't), but I thought that as long as Callas was in town, I might as well see the other two. Maybe she would do something I liked better.

Just for the record, she performed *Norma* on stage eighty-four times, far more than any other role. She had revived this difficult and demanding Bellini opera and made it her own, along with other difficult and demanding bel canto operas that she brought back from obscurity and restored to the repertoire. Good for her, good for opera, but not good for me.

I thought her second Chicago opera, *La Traviata*, was a great improvement. It was even a familiar story, thanks to Greta Garbo's movie *Camille* with Robert Taylor as the hero and Lionel Barrymore as the hero's dominating father. This was Verdi, at least a familiar name, and there were a number of nifty tunes. Things were looking up.

Her last opera was Donizetti's *Lucia*. I had never seen or heard anything like it. Neither had Chicago. At the end of her tremendous long mad scene, when she came out on stage for her curtain call, still in her blood-stained nightgown, preserving that sad, dazed expression, the audience went berserk. Wild applause and whistles and shouts. Middle-aged Chicago businessmen and their wives came storming down the aisles to get as close as possible to that magic figure with the magic voice.

From that night on, and ever since, I have loved opera — and Maria Callas.

When I finished my Chicago bureau stint, I came back to New York as an editor in the Articles Department. One of the first stories I suggested was a full-length article on Callas and what made her such a worldwide success. The article ran with the title "Voice of an Angel." I didn't write it, I only assigned and edited it, but Callas knew it was my idea and my story, and she sent me a warm message of thanks. The article more than made up for the Chicago fiasco.

While I did not see Callas again for several years, I listened to her recordings, and I kept track of her through the many press stories about her. They were mostly unfavorable, not so much about her voice as about her impossible behavior. Time after time there was some new Callas scandal — broken dates, fights with general managers and conductors, wars with tenors, obstreperous demands for this and that.

I knew Callas only from that brief time in Chicago, but I found all those stories hard to believe. She was not only a great singer but a profoundly serious professional.

What was this all about? I thought it would be interesting to hear her side of the story.

So I called her up at her house in Milan.

Callas often said in interviews that the voice in opera should not always be beautiful. Depending on the situation and the character, sometimes the voice should be harsh, bitter, angry — yes, even ugly.

She certainly carried that over into her telephone voice. When she answered her own phone, as she often did, her voice was sharp, nasal, nasty. Perhaps she was expecting an antagonistic reporter with some rude question, as no doubt frequently happened. But as soon as she realized it was a friend, her voice softened.

I made my pitch. How would she like to tell her version of all those Callas scandals that the world was reading about? We would pay our top fee (about what she got for a performance in a major opera house). I would fly to Milan, we would do the story together, but this would not be presented as an interview. It would be her story under her own byline, and she would have control of every word. I hoped there would be a LIFE cover, though I couldn't promise that.

Immediate enthusiasm. She was furious about all those one-sided stories, full of lies and misinterpretations and mistakes. She did not even mention the fee. (Her position on fees for performances was, I thought, very reasonable, given her stature. She did not ask to be paid more than anybody else at any given opera house, but she did not want to be paid less than anybody else.) Now then, straight to business. How soon could we do it? Let me get my calendar.

We made a date, and I flew to Milan. Although as a

teenager I had lived in the Philippines, and then served around the Pacific during World War II, this was my first trip to Europe. I was very nervous. I spoke no Italian. Our Rome bureau chief, my good friend Dodie Hamblin, who made all my travel and hotel arrangements, told me I had nothing to worry about. "With the Italians, just keep smiling, and they'll work things out for you. It's different with the French."

Callas lived in an elegant townhouse with her husband, Giovanni Battista Meneghini, a wealthy, much older Milanese businessman who had given up his business to become her manager. Our long talks took place in the bright, richly decorated living room, Callas on a couch, me in a chair with notebook and pencil. By now we were "Maria" and "Ralph." In New York, sorting through all the press clippings in the Callas morgue folder, I had selected nine Callas scandals to discuss. I had deliberately not told her ahead of time which ones they were because I wanted to hear her fresh, unprepared response.

Her response and her memory of precise details were extraordinary. She had long been known for her fabulous memory, enabling her to learn and perform many more lead roles than most sopranos. She had once, under deadline pressure, learned the entire lead role of Elvira in *I Puritani* in six days. Even so, her recall for details of the "scandals" amazed me — names, dates, time of day, locations, dialogue, contractual clauses, even facial expressions and gestures. But that was not what most impressed me. The great thing about our talks was her candor, her vigor and frequently her anger. She was outspoken about everything and everybody. Yes, of course it was self-serving, but it was convincing. And what shone through everything she said was her fierce commitment to excellence. In her intense inner world, a poor performance was not just unacceptable, it was damnable.

I was having a great time — and so was she.

When we broke for lunch, she asked me what I would like to drink. Back home I would have asked for a martini, but I thought I would show Maria how soigné I could be, here in Milan. I asked for a Compari and soda, a very Italian drink that I didn't much like. I failed to impress her.

"Ugh!" she said, "How can you stand that bitter stuff?"

Lunch was a revelation. At a long dining room table there were four of us. Down at the far end was Meneghini, a balding, white-haired gentleman several inches shorter than his wife. I sat in the middle of the table, and at the near end sat Maria, who served as translator during the lunch because Meneghini spoke no English. And right next to Maria, erect, silent, perfectly poised on a chair, sat her toy poodle. During our simple spaghetti lunch, during which nothing else of interest took place, Maria occasionally picked a bit of pasta from her plate with her fingers and fed it to the poodle. It is not easy to handle floppy spaghetti, but both Maria and the poodle did so. I could see why the poodle was a success, but I found it hard to understand what Callas saw in Meneghini. (And indeed, she later dumped him for Aristotle Onassis, who in turn dumped her for Jackie Kennedy, whom he in turn later divorced. Many losers, although Jackie got a vast settlement.)

After lunch, on with the interview all afternoon. Back in those days, 1959, very few reporters used tape recorders, so I don't have a taped record of what she said and how she said it. But it was the best interview I ever had, not just for content but also for tone of voice and vividness of expression. I knew it would be easy to write, and it was.

Back in my hotel room I typed out her story, working fast and steadily. She had been quite reckless in some of the things she said about her colleagues, both singers and conductors and administrators, so our libel lawyers were bound to have a number of problems. You know you have a good story if the lawyers are worried.

When I finished, a long story of some five thousand words, I delivered the manuscript directly to Maria at her front door. She looked excited and expectant. I told her I was going to visit our Rome bureau for two days, so she would have time to read it and make any corrections she thought necessary. I told her I thought it was terrific.

"Good," she said, "and I will translate it for my husband."

"Good," I said, not knowing any better.

When I came back from Rome, Maria handed me a completely retyped manuscript. "My husband had a few suggestions," she explained.

I sat down in her living room and read the new manuscript with increasing, and finally, total dismay. All the juice, all the fire, all the excitement were gone. What took their place was a lot of sanctimonious pap about her "Art" and her "Devotion to Music."

Until now we had always been on her turf, but now we were on mine. I told her, "Maria, LIFE won't publish this."

She acted surprised, but then she was the best actress in opera. I'm not sure how surprised she really was. "Why not?"

I was so angry at what had happened to this wonderful story that I made no pretence of kindness. I told her that what she had done had destroyed the piece, and I explained why, in detail.

She listened carefully. At the end she said, "My husband didn't want me to annoy people. He says I already have enough enemies."

"Well, if you want your story in LIFE, this is definitely not it. Are you willing to fix it?"

We spent the next two days negotiating, paragraph by paragraph. I kept trying to restore the original, and Meneghini, arguing with Maria in Italian, kept dragging his feet.

I got rid of almost all of the sanctimonious insertions, and I got back about half of the original material, although some of the names and savage details were either toned down or omitted altogether. But at least, given who she was, it was now a piece LIFE would be glad to publish. And so we did.

But first came the pictures.

I was back in New York when the black-and-white pictures were taken. They were fine and, along with some pictures of past events, would illustrate her story. Now for the cover, which had to be in color.

Not only did I and Maria want a cover. So did the Managing Editor Ed Thompson, who liked the story and had learned a lot about Callas since he had minimized the story on her American debut.

The pictures came in. They were stiff. Shot in profile,

her nose looked even more prominent. Not a chance. We sent a cable asking for a second take.

The pictures came in, still stiff. It is strange that Callas, who could be so electrifying and expressive on stage and in her music, froze up in front of a still camera. If you look at the pictures on all her opera CDs, the only good ones are taken from a performance and in costume. When it's a straight portrait, there is nothing there.

Along with the second set of cover tries, my friend Dodie Hamblin in Rome passed along something Callas had said to the photographer. "Those big fat men with cigars will probably pick a movie star."

With these pictures, even I couldn't argue for a Callas cover. Ed Thompson was not fat but certainly hefty, and he did smoke cigars. The cover for the issue of April 20, 1959, containing the Callas story, was a sexy close-up of Marilyn Monroe chewing on a pearl necklace.

I saw Maria's final performance at the Metropolitan Opera in *Tosca*, one of her most popular roles, on March 25, 1965. She was still a great actress, and Tosca is one of the best acting roles in opera, but the great voice was gone, worn out by too many performances of too many roles for too many years. Even as inexpert an ear as mine could tell that she should never have taken this on. At one shrieking note the audience gasped.

I had hoped to at last introduce my wife to Callas, and we had tickets to the celebration dinner party in the beautiful Pool Room at the Four Seasons. Callas did not show up. I couldn't blame her.

That sounds like a sad ending to a great career, but the

real ending was better. In 1972 she came to New York's Juilliard School of Music to teach a dozen Master Classes to young operatic hopefuls. A few journalists were allowed to attend, and they were unanimous in their praise for her kindness, sympathy and encouragement toward her students. This reality was a far cry from the hit Broadway play *Master Class,* which depicted her beating up mercilessly on three students. In the long record of misrepresentations of Callas, this play was perhaps the most vicious as well as the most unfair. But by that time Callas was dead and could no longer fight back.

I saw Maria for the last time at the end of her Master Classes. I took her to lunch in the Oak Room at the Plaza. She looked the same, even though the voice had gone. She wore a strong-colored red dress and a pillbox fur hat, possibly mink but I'd bet it was sable. We did not talk about old times but about her Master Classes. She said how much she had enjoyed teaching and that she had tried to instill in her students the dedication that she had always felt.

I asked her what was the main thing she tried to teach them.

She suddenly leaned toward me and put her hand on my forearm. It was the first time in eighteen years that there had been any touch except a handshake. She gripped my arm hard as though to ensure that this was something to remember. Her big eyes were intense.

"Discipline," she said, pounding the word. "Discipline, Ralph. Everything is discipline."

I will tell you a Callas story about discipline. It is also about courage. And about showmanship. It took place at

Milan's La Scala in a performance of *La Traviata* in 1955, when Callas was still at her peak. Also at its peak was the rivalry between Callas and Renata Tebaldi, two giant so-pranos performing in constant competition, with ardent devotees on both sides.

The boxes at La Scala run down almost to the stage, and on this night the box nearest the stage had been cap-tured by Tebaldi fans. All through the opening act, when-ever Callas sang, groans and even laughter came from the box. It was so disruptive that members of the audience were looking toward the box and making hushing sounds and gestures. The disruption continued. Everybody was aware of it and annoyed, most of all Callas herself.

When the moment came for Violetta's great double aria at the end of Act I, *Ah fors'e lui* and *Sempre libera*, she stepped out of the role, walked to the front of the stage right beneath the box and sang straight to the box. Arms at her side, no gestures. This is a long, complex piece of music. Everybody in the Italian audience knew exactly what she was doing. This is Babe Ruth pointing to the centerfield bleachers and promising a home run. If Callas did not hit that home run, if she made one mis-take, she was dead. The audience held its breath through those eight minutes of intricate, demanding music. Per-fect all the way through, and when she hit those last two high notes to perfection, the audience exploded. Home run! Home run! Brava! Brava! The whole audience stand-ing and applauding and cheering, not just for the perfec-tion but for the incredible gamble.

Callas did not move. She stood still, arms still at her sides, staring up at the box. This only provoked the au-dience to greater applause that went on and on and on. At last, Callas turned to the audience and gave a single deep bow of appreciation. Then she turned back to the box, held up her right arm and, in the immemorial Italian gesture of triumph and contempt, she shook her clenched fist.

Several years ago the Metropolitan's magazine *Opera News* conducted a poll of experts on the question of who had the most beautiful voice. Among the sopranos, Callas did not get one single vote. Her voice, even during her greatest decade, never had the pure, crystal beauty of Tebaldi or Elizabeth Schwarzkopf or Kiri Te Kanawa or today's Renee Fleming.

For Callas it was the wrong question. If the poll had asked who was the greatest actress in the history of opera, or who performed the most leading roles (forty-three on stage, four more in recordings), or who brought back the most once-forgotten operas, or who had the greatest impact on opera since Enrico Caruso, there would have been no contest. Maria Callas would have won them all.

CHARLES LINDBERGH

Charles Lindbergh entered my life when I was three years old, although he would not know about it until some forty years later.

In all American history, starting with the landings at Jamestown and Plymouth Rock, we have never had such a perfect hero as Lindbergh. And I'm not sure that the rest of the world in the rest of history has anything better to offer. His solo flight across the Atlantic, New York to Paris in May 1927, electrified the world. The achievement itself would have been more than enough, even if he had been old, ugly and nasty. But he wasn't. He was tall, young, lanky and handsome, not in some slick Hollywood or Broadway fashion but in a natural, casual, Midwestern way. He even had a perfect casual nickname, Slim. After the flight he was promoted to "The Lone Eagle" and "Lucky Lindy," although luck had nothing to do with it. Every time he smiled or spoke, he was worth a picture or a story. It would be impossible to invent such a hero.

My parents were as captivated as everybody else. Lindbergh made a post-flight tour in his single-engine monoplane, *Spirit of St. Louis*. It was already — and still is — the most famous plane in aviation history. You can see it today, remarkably small, hanging from the ceiling of the Smithsonian Museum. One of his tour stops was Washington, D.C. My parents, especially my father who was an editor at the *National Geographic*, thought I must see this event, even though I was too young to understand or appreciate it. It was the same motivation that made me, in 1969, wake up my young daughter, Sara, and hold her in my lap at two in the morning so that she could see, and perhaps remember, Neil Armstrong step down onto the moon.

I have a hazy memory, not amounting to much, of being in a huge crowd of people, on a bright sunny day, and being held aloft by my father so that I could see, far in the distance — whatever it was. A tiny plane? I don't remember. I certainly did not see Lindbergh himself, although I suppose he must have been out there somewhere.

When I was a bit older, I discovered that I hated my middle name, Augustus.

Since I had been christened a junior — Ralph Augustus Graves, Jr. — I was stuck with it, but that didn't mean I liked it. I complained that it was a fancy, sissy name. My parents said I should really be proud of it because I had the same middle name as the great Charles Augustus Lindbergh.

Many years pass during which Lindbergh and I have no discernible impact on each other.

In 1949 he was put on my list of famous people from the Twenties to pose for our Mid-Century Issue (see Philippe Halsman chapter). Nobody took that listing seriously. Ever since the kidnapping and murder of his baby son and the raucous, interminable trial that followed, the

Lindberghs had shunned the press. Never an interview, never a picture. Their phone number was not only unlisted, but trusted friends who knew the number were told never to give it out. On the opening page of our big color essay on the twenties figures, we ran a small black-and-white picture of Lindbergh, shot when he was making a speech in support of the isolationist group America First, probably the most unpopular thing he ever did.

Our paths crossed again — sort of — in the early 1950s when I was LIFE's Chicago bureau chief. This was a heavy-drinking, loud-singing collection of correspondents and photographers who often partied together. Late in the evening when the boisterous singing started, after "The Sloop John B." and "I Want to Say Hello, I Want to See You Smile," we always wound up with the 1920's Lindbergh song. It begins "Lindbergh, oh what a flying fool was he," and it ends with "So take your hats off to plucky, lucky Lindbergh, the eagle of the USA." We always pretended to raise nonexistent hats as we finished.

It is perhaps time to get down to our first meeting.

At the end of each year LIFE published a special double issue, two issues in one devoted to a single major subject. This had its origin in the crassest commercial motives. The regular weekly LIFE issues at Christmas and New Year's always lost money because of skimpy ad pages, and newsstand sales were poor during the holiday season. The pre-Christmas advertising was over, and the next year's ad programs had not yet begun. Well, why not combine those two losing issues into one big issue devoted to a single subject? It would save both printing and mailing costs to do one issue instead of two, and maybe we could convince advertisers that they should be represented in such a very special issue.

It worked superbly. Advertisers did sign up, so our ad salesmen were happy. The editors loved it because they could do expansive stories on a favorite subject. The issue sold well on the newsstands, even at an increased price, so the Circulation Department was happy. Because we were both saving money and making money, the publisher was happy. There was, of course, intense competition each year between edit departments as to what the subject should be. In 1967, after I had lobbied heavily on behalf of my favorite Nature Department and on the environmental movement for preservation, I was put in charge of the special double issue called The Wild World, with a wide-eared African elephant on the cover. As an assistant managing editor, I had been doing many stories on the environment, a hot new cause in the sixties, and I wanted environmental stories in the Wild World. The much-endangered whale seemed a fine subject for such an article.

I was aware that Charles Lindbergh had also become an outspoken defender and promoter of the environment and that one of his causes was the whale. What a perfect author for what a perfect subject! But how to reach him to propose it?

A former managing editor of *Time* and an ardent aviation devotee from World War II days was a man named Roy Alexander. He was known to know Lindbergh. When I told him about our project and asked if he would tell us how to get in touch with Lindbergh, he said no, he would not. But the whale article might interest his friend. If I would write down what we wanted, he would get it to Lindbergh.

David Maness, who had succeeded me as articles editor when I was promoted, helped compose the letter. We
had to describe the special issue, explain how environ-
mentally conscious it would be, describe what we wanted
to say about whales and why we wanted Lindbergh to
say it. We both signed it and gave both our phone numbers. I gave Roy Alexander the letter and hoped for the
best — but not with very much hope.

A few days later Dave Maness's phone rang. When he
said hello, a voice said, "This is General Lindbergh."
Dave told me he felt a huge chill of excitement.

Lindbergh had read our letter, found it interesting and
suggested that we have a meeting. He would like to bring
his wife, Anne, and he had an idea. Dave Maness bab-
bled yes, yes, yes, and they set a date. Dave knew that
whatever I might have scheduled, I would cancel it for
this.

In addition to his recent involvement in the environment, Lindbergh had been active in many ways. In World
War II, in the guise of a forty-year-old "civilian test pilot,"
he had flown some fifty combat missions in the Pacific
and had taught young fighter pilots how to conserve gas
and greatly extend the range of their missions. After the
war he became a high-level consultant for both Pan American Airways and Boeing. He took time to write the complete, accurate and vividly told story of his epic 1927
flight to Paris, and that book, *The Spirit of St. Louis,* won
the Pulitzer Prize. Because of his many contributions to
aviation, President Eisenhower restored him to military
rank as a brigadier general in the Air Force Reserve. One
year after Lindbergh's Pulitzer his wife, Anne Morrow
Lindbergh, wrote *Gift from the Sea,* an early and poetic

feminist book that became the country's number one best seller.

We met the Lindberghs in the privacy of Maness's office behind closed doors. Lindbergh could still have gone by his old nickname Slim. Tall, a couple of inches over six feet, he was every inch a brigadier general in the Reserve. A balding forehead, but otherwise looking much younger than his sixty-five years. Perfectly relaxed and casual, right from the start, as though he had known us for years. Anne Morrow Lindbergh was small and small-faced, pretty, even slimmer than Slim, dark-haired and extremely quiet. Both then and in the later times when I saw them together, she preferred that he do the talking. She was not stiff but reserved, a most private person.

They sat side by side on the office couch facing Dave and me in chairs. The general opened by congratulating us on what we were doing in the Wild World issue. He also, to my extreme delight, congratulated us on our recent environmental news stories, especially those showing the damage to wildlife and shorelines caused by oil spills. Now about the whales. An excellent subject, and he was pleased that we had thought of asking him, but he could not take the time just now. However, he and Anne had a suggestion. Their son Jon, an oceanographer, a graduate specialist, was very interested in whales and knew a lot about them. He had even gone swimming with whales under water. Why not ask him to do the story? Jon was not a writer, but his parents would be willing to help him.

We all four agreed to try it. As the meeting ended, Lindbergh gave us his phone number. The meeting had been so pleasant and friendly that I could say, "I thought you never gave out your phone number."

Lindbergh smiled. He still had a great smile, just a few decades older than when he landed in Paris. He said, "When we decide to trust somebody, we trust them completely."

Dave Maness took over the Jon Lindbergh article. A fair amount of rewrite work had to be done by Dave and by Jon, with perhaps some help from his parents. In the Wild World issue it was not as wonderful as Romain Gary's brilliant tribute to the elephant, an eloquent long letter addressed to "Dear Elephant, Sir," or as the Desmond Morris book excerpt called "The Human Animal," but it was a solid article on an important subject.

Best of all, it began my long and happy association with Lindbergh.

For the next five years we were constantly in touch about environmental stories. Sometimes he would suggest a story. Sometimes I would suggest the story and ask him for advice or access. We had private lunches and exchanged letters and phone calls. Somewhere along the way I got around to calling him Charles instead of General. He was very interested in the primitive tribes and wildlife of the Philippines, and when I told him that I had spent high school years in the Philippines and served there in World War II, we spent a lot of time talking about that country. We talked about the possibility of going there together some day

He gave me his book about the great flight, written completely in the present tense and ending just as he lands his plane at the Paris airport. After I had read it, I asked him what his first words had been after landing. In other accounts I had read, "Well, we made it," and "I'd like a glass of milk." Did he say either of those? Or something else? Did he remember? He laughed and said he certainly did remember. The last sentence of his book reads, "I start to taxi back toward the floodlights and the hangars — But the entire field ahead is covered with running figures!" He told me that those figures swarmed around his plane, touching it, rocking it, getting as close as they could to this fantastic historical moment.

"I was afraid they were going to wreck my plane," he said. "So my first words were, 'Are there any guards?' Not very heroic."

Back to that Wild World Special Issue. Most of the stories had already closed, but because of something he had said during one of our talks, I had a last-minute thought.

He had told me that in spite of the enormous advances in science and technology, in which he had played a considerable part, he was more and more struck by the crucial importance of the natural world, the wild world, that had so much to teach us.

I asked him if he would be willing to write a short piece on that subject. I would use it to introduce my special issue. He wrote back that unfortunately he had no time to write such a piece — and then added a lengthy, detailed letter giving his thoughts on the subject.

I read the letter again. Then I called him up and asked him if I could just run his letter as a signed article. He did not pause long, so I suspect he had thought of this before I did. Yes.

"Great," I said. And to illustrate the article, which we called "The Wisdom of Wildness," could we run the photograph he had shown me that was taken on his recent trip to the Krakatoa volcano in Indonesia. He thought longer about that because he was still, after all these years, ducking photographic publicity. But at last he said yes, and we ran the picture with his article. He is standing in profile on the slopes of the volcano, wearing an open-necked shirt and casual slacks. I think it was the first picture he had approved for publication in many years. He looked great.

During one of our lunches I told him the childhood story about my middle name Augustus, how much I had hated it, and how my parents had tried to placate me by saying it was also Lindbergh's middle name.

"Charles," I asked, "when you were growing up, how did you feel about having Augustus as a middle name?"

He smiled and shrugged. "You can get used to almost anything."

MICHAEL ARLEN

Michael Arlen was more fun to talk to than anybody I have ever known. Although he was a witty conversationalist, and although I listened to him for many hours over many lunches, and although I have an excellent memory, only a handful of his quotes survive. But I do have a perfect excuse. Actually, two perfect excuses.

Sid James, the assistant managing in charge of LIFE's News Department, had known Michael Arlen for some years, both in Los Angeles and New York. Arlen often talked about manners, both good manners and bad manners, and James kept urging him to write a piece about manners for LIFE. Arlen refused. He didn't need the money, and he had given up writing. James kept after him. Finally Arlen said, "Send me one of your bright young men, and I will talk it to him."

Sid James picked me. At the time I was writing picture stories for the magazine: textblocks, captions, headlines and subheads. I was pretty good at it, but so were half a dozen other bright young men. I think James may have picked me because I had published a novel, so maybe there would be some chemistry. I had never heard of Arlen. James explained who he was.

Michael Arlen was only a pen name that he had

picked out of the air. An Armenian with some long, un-pronounceable name, born in Bulgaria but growing up in England, he had become a wildly successful fiction writer in the 1920s. In 1927 he made the cover of *Time*. He was the Scott Fitzgerald of England, writing novels and short stories about the British upper social classes in London's Mayfair. Like Fitzgerald, he had become a recognized figure in his own milieu, part of his fictional society, always nattily dressed, zipping around London in his yellow Rolls Royce. His work was witty and cynical but romantic enough to capture a wide popular following. His most famous book was *The Green Hat,* which became a successful London play with Tallulah Bankhead and a successful silent movie with Greta Garbo. I had never heard of that, either. James said this was understandable. Arlen had made all his money long ago and then quit writing.

We met for the first time — and for many times thereafter — at the King Cole Bar on the first floor of the St. Regis Hotel, 5th Avenue and 55th Street. This is six blocks away — a crucial six blocks, as we shall see — from the Time-Life Building in Rockefeller Center. The King Cole Bar did indeed have a long bar below the famous Old King Cole mural by Maxfield Parrish, but it also had a spacious dining room, for men only at lunch.

The corner round table across the room from the mural, just inside the main entrance, belonged to Michael Arlen. It was reserved for him at lunch, Monday through Friday, unless he phoned ahead to release it. And there he sat, his hands folded over what looked to me like a silver-headed cane. He shook hands with us sitting down, first with Sid, then with me. This did not strike me as perfect manners from the man who was going to teach me about manners, but as he later explained, if he stood up every time someone stopped by his table to say hello, lunch would become "not only interminable but exhausting."

The word *dapper* was invented for Michael Arlen. His blue silk tie was perfectly knotted, his shirt gleaming white with starched collar, a dark, expensive-looking suit — surely made for him in London? His curly gray-black hair was short and neatly trimmed. So was his mustache. His full eyebrows were black. He was a bit under medium height, lean and handsome in a vaguely Oriental way. Now in his early fifties he was, as he once boasted about himself, "every other inch a gentleman."

I don't recall what we ate, but we all had martinis, the customary drink of that day. Sid and Arlen talked about old times and old acquaintances. Turning to me, Arlen said he understood that I had written a novel. What was it called? How did it do? I told him it was a college novel called *Thanks for the Ride* and it had sold only 1,800 copies. He smiled and said he could have at least doubled my sales with a better title, but he didn't say what the title might have been. He asked if I was writing another novel. I said yes of course, and he nodded approval.

Nobody had anything to say about manners. At the end of the lunch, which Sid paid for on behalf of LIFE, he said that after this he would leave it to Michael and me to do the story, if that was okay with Michael. Arlen said fine, so I guess I had passed. Arlen and I made a date for lunch — same time, same place, how about next Tuesday?

On Tuesday we did talk a bit about manners but not too much. He pointed out that if a person was taking a walk on the shady Central Park side of Fifth Avenue, it would be bad manners to greet him, interrupting what was plainly a solitary walk. But if that person was walking on the sunny, busy side of Fifth, then it would be good manners to greet him because he was plainly open to conversation. I was not convinced, but I remembered it.

On my own I had decided that it would be bad manners for me to take notes when I was lunching with such an elegant man in such an elegant setting. Instead I would rely on my good memory. But I had not allowed for the fact that Arlen turned out to be a particularly devoted martini drinker, and I considered it good manners to keep pace with him. He even had a name for each martini. The first was Daisy, the second was Maude, and the third was Robinson. As a teenage boy in England, he had been hopelessly enamored of two lovely little sisters named Daisy and Maude. But he was prevented from making any romantic progress because they were protected by their governess, a fierce figure named Robinson. So "Robinson" prevented Arlen from having a fourth martini at lunch.

That did not provide such a strict protection as this charming story might lead one to think. After our three martinis and a light lunch ("Food interferes with conversation, alcohol does not"), Arlen might summon the head waiter, an unctuous fellow who reminded me of a husky Uriah Heep, and said, "Bert, bring us a glass of your filthy port."

After these lunches I would walk slowly and carefully down Fifth Avenue, trying to remember one or at most two quotes until I reached my office. That's one of my two excuses for not being able to recall more Arlen quotes.

The next time we had lunch, and we quickly settled on

a weekly lunch, always paid for by LIFE, Arlen brought me a copy of *The Green Hat*, which he thought I might be amused to read, and would I please return it. It was the lurid story of Iris March who, the first paragraph tells us, wore a green hat *pour le sport*. We are then treated to sexual scandals, suicide, syphilis, etc. Tallulah and Garbo must have had a romp.

In the course of many lunches Arlen, at my request, brought me one of his books after another until I believe I read them all. They were dated, to be sure, but most were at least amusing and at best enjoyable. I asked him why he had stopped writing. He said that he knew, unlike most writers, when his time had passed. What he had written with great success in the Jazz Age twenties no longer felt right in the Depression thirties. He had never written for literary fame. He had written for fun and especially for money. He told me that at the height of his popularity, a European multimillionaire (sorry, name lost during one of those post-martini walks down Fifth Avenue) had asked him, "Michael, what would you do if I offered you a million dollars for all the profits from everything you write from now on?" Arlen told him it would be a very bad investment, "because I would never write another word."

While Arlen and I were lunching and talking, many people would stop to say hello to him. Once in a great while he would ask the person to join us. That is how I once had a long and lively lunch with John O'Hara. Arlen said that most writers were, contrary to common belief, very good talkers. Over the years he had entertained and enjoyed many of them at this table. The major exception, he said, was Somerset Maugham. Willie, Arlen said, would sit here and never say a word while everybody else was trying to be the wittiest and quickest. His silence had nothing to do with his famous stammer, Arlen said with scorn. Willie was memorizing so that he could use the brilliant dialogue in his next story. I thought that if that was indeed Willie's aim, he probably didn't have three martinis and a glass of filthy port.

Eventually I stopped calling him Mr. Arlen and switched to Michael. He also took me home once to meet his gorgeous wife, Atalanta, a Greek countess.

I can't say how many lunches it took me to decide that the LIFE article should not be about manners. It should be about Michael Arlen himself, the writer who knew when to quit. As we know, even great writers tend to write on and on, past their excellence and down into their decadence. Hemingway is perhaps the most notorious example. But Arlen had had his heyday, and he knew when it was over.

I wrote a lighthearted article, my first for LIFE, and the Articles Department liked it. It was filled with all the good quotes I had painstakingly collected. It was scheduled to close, as our articles always did, on Thursday afternoon. Unfortunately, Luce held his editors lunch that day, and, unfortunately, he asked Cal Whipple of the Articles Department what LIFE's article was going to be. Whipple answered that it was an amusing piece about Michael Arlen.

"That old has-been?" Luce asked in disbelief. "That's no good. What else have you got?"

So my piece didn't run, then or ever. Later when I tried to find a copy, just for the record, it had disappeared. That's my second perfect excuse for not having more

Arlen quotes. When I told Michael what had happened to the story, he smiled and shrugged. Then he said, "I sat next to Luce at dinner once. He struck me as a man who wanted to talk about sex but didn't dare."

Michael and I, on the other hand, often talked about women and sex, although not in a prurient way. I remember one quote that I didn't put in my article because we were supposed to be "a family magazine." He said, "A man of my age is, let's face it, fighting a rather squalid rearguard action against impotence." I remember it because it's my favorite use of the word *squalid*.

In early 1956 I got a call from his wife, Atalanta. We barely knew each other.

She said Michael wanted me to know that he was very ill and would not be able to come to lunch. He had lung cancer. It was very difficult for him to talk. I wrote him a letter saying how hugely I had enjoyed our many lunches together, and I hoped he would recover so that we could have many more.

A month or so later I got another phone call from Atalanta. Michael was much worse, but he wanted to see me again. I offered to come to their apartment, but she said no, Michael and I had always met at the King Cole, so that's where he would like to see me. She would bring him. Of course, women were not allowed in the King Cole Bar, but there was a small room close by that we could use for the meeting. We set the time.

They were already there, seated, when I arrived. I don't remember the room at all. He looked terrible, as dying men do. He had lost a lot of weight, his neck was scrawny with deep vertical wrinkles, and his face was pale. But his hair and mustache were neatly trimmed. His tie, around the shirt collar that was now too large for him, was as neatly knotted as always. Atalanta had to have done all this for him because he was too weak to have done it himself. He would have insisted that it all look just so.

I sat down in front of him and took both his hands and held them.

"It hurts him to talk," Atalanta said. "He just wanted to see you."

Michael nodded, then began to cry, very softly, holding himself in, but the tears trickled down his face. We looked at each other.

I knew he was crying for himself, for what was happening to him, as well as crying for us and for our many good times that were now over. I kept holding his hands, and then I cried too. For the first time, we had nothing to say.

A MONSTROUS NIGHT
AT THE WHITE HOUSE

I was never a newsman. I never worked in LIFE's big News Department that produced most of the lead stories each week and many of the covers. I never worked in our Washington bureau, so I never reported on or wrote about any of the eight American presidents who held office during my long career. but, as the assistant managing editor responsible for all LIFE's articles, I did spend one extraordinary five-hour, intimate evening in the White House with that monstrous figure, President Lyndon Johnson.

By *monstrous* I don't mean, in dictionary terms, either "ugly or frightening appearance" or "inhumanly or outrageously evil," although severe critics would disagree. What I do mean is "extremely and dauntingly large." I can't remember anyone I ever met who seemed so much larger than life.

I and several of my colleagues were summoned to Washington in the spring of 1964 because of an investigative story we were doing on the President's finances, both LBJ's and his wife, Lady Bird's. Our top investigative reporter William Lambert had been digging and scouring and interviewing for months, and our veteran staff writer

Keith Wheeler had written up Lambert's findings in a long, scathing two-part article that we were now ready to publish. It was full of fascinating Texas-style shenanigans and insider political deals, and we knew it was going to make a front-page fuss. So did the White House.

The summons came by telephone to me from the office of Abe Fortas, LBJ's personal lawyer, longtime friend and future appointee to the Supreme Court. (Fortas would later be forced to resign from the Court because of another investigative LIFE story by the same William Lambert.) The White House knew all about our prospective story and demanded that we appear to discuss it in detail.

This was important enough for me to notify Henry Luce. Actually, I was hoping he would tell me we didn't have to go to Washington — freedom of the press and all that — but he said that of course I had to obey a presidential summons. Be sure to let him know what happened. He was much calmer about it than I was, but then he had dealt with many presidents and I had dealt with none.

Our team consisted of me, the authors Lambert and Wheeler, Articles Editor Dave Maness and our Washington bureau chief Richard Stolley. We all showed up at five in the afternoon in the law offices of Abe Fortas near Dupont Circle. A small, thin, slim-faced man in his fifties, he rose from behind his desk to shake hands with each of us. On his desk were two steep stacks of folders filled with papers. When we were all seated, he explained that these stacks contained complete information and documentation of all the Johnson financial holdings. Absolutely everything, nothing withheld. Because of all the misinformation that he knew LIFE had been collecting, the president had authorized Fortas to answer any questions we might have and to furnish documented proof of the answers.

But we had no questions. Lambert's and Wheeler's work had been exhaustive and was now complete.

Fortas spent half an hour trying to solicit questions, chiefly from Lambert. He kept offering to discuss subject areas — radio and television holdings in Texas, forest holdings in Alabama — but Lambert said we were satisfied that we already had accurate information.

Fortas, acknowledging the impasse, said that he would have to call the president. He did so in our presence, giving a brief, accurate, dispassionate summary of our conversation. A pause, then a "Yes, sir," then he hung up.

"The President would like to see us in the White House in an hour." He looked at his watch. "I will meet you downstairs in forty-five mintues with a limousine."

The five-hour meeting took place in the family dining room on the second floor of the White House. A long, bare, polished dark wooden table, chairs down the sides with one chair at each end. The President, seated at the head, rose when we walked in and shook hands with each of us. A huge, firm handclasp, a direct stare into each face. Very tall, a dominant figure, the voice still full of Texas, in spite of all his years in Washington.

To demonstrate how little I knew about the protocol of official meetings, I failed to take the seat next to the president which, as the senior LIFE editor present I should have done. I was ignorant but lucky. Our bureau chief

Dick Stolley wound up in that seat. During that long evening, time after time the President leaned forward to emphasize a point and grasped Stolley hard on thigh or forearm. Next morning Stolley had bruises on his right arm and leg.

Across from Stolley on the President's right was Fortas, and next to him were Wheeler and Lambert. Maness sat next to me. Down at the far end, for no discernible reason, completely silent throughout the meeting, was the President's aide Walter Jenkins, who would later be dismissed because of a homosexual scandal in a men's bathroom.

As opposed to the stacks of folders that had cluttered Fortas's law-office desk, the only document in sight was a sheaf of standard-size sheets of paper stapled together. It lay on the dining room table at Johnson's right hand. When he picked it up, we could see that the typewritten pages were single-spaced flimsy carbons rather than originals.

Johnson made an elaborate show of going through those pages. The whole evening would be one long performance. Here he is, president of the United States, with the Vietnam War and the country and the whole world on his mind, but right now he has all the time in the world for this crucial matter of his personal reputation.

With the sheets in hand he looked around the table at each of us. Then he carefully licked a forefinger and turned a page and looked at it. Then he looked around at us again, licked his finger again, and turned another page. Finally, he said, "This is a report on all the people you been talking to about my money. And my wife's money. They are my enemies, so I know every lie they told you."

He tossed the sheaf back on the table and never referred to it again. He looked at us slowly, one by one. The mournful eyes, the long head, the powerful nose, the big long ears. "Gentlemen," he said, with ponderous sincerity, "I'm the only President you got."

He explained that if the one and only President was falsely accused or misrepresented in the public press, the country itself would be damaged because the public would lose faith in its leader. Criticism was different. He expected criticism, every man in politics expects that, he never minded honest criticism. But *false* criticism, *false* facts, that is terrible. The press has a sacred duty to avoid that, especially when it comes to the President himself.

And we must not think that we could print something false that he or his press secretary could simply deny. He shook his head, dead serious. In politics, he said, you never deny.

Then without a pause he switched from this solemn analysis to a vulgar Texas yarn. I could not believe this came straight from the President's mouth to a group of journalists he didn't even know. I repeated it several times the next day and many times in the years since. This is just what he said:

Back home in Texas there was this young feller running for office for the first time. Nice-looking young feller, nice way of talking, but he didn't know first thing about campaigning, and he was running against a tough incumbent. But he had this smart old adviser. The adviser told him, "Son, you going to make just one speech in this campaign. Every speech you going to say just one thing. You going to say your opponent, the incumbent, fucks hogs." Young feller gets all excited, all pink in the ears, and he says, "Is that *true*?" And the old adviser says, "No, son, it isn't. But you just keep on saying it. And if you can get him to deny it just once, you will be elected!"

Huge bellow from the President, a grasp of Stolley's thigh, laughs from all of us.

Drawing the lesson from his homily, he said that no matter what we published, he was not going to deny it. No matter how wrong it is. "So get it right *before* you publish."

He glared around the table. "Ask me a question. I got nothing to hide. I'll take down my pants, I'll show you my pecker. But don't you write that it's nine inches long if you're too lazy to look. Ask me a question!"

For some time he continued to invite questions, though in less colorful language.

Finally — I suspect out of kindness to the only President we got — Bill Lambert asked several little questions about a minor aspect of his investigation. The President leapt to answer in detail, but when he finished, the question period died away.

Johnson must have realized that nothing was going to come of this. Perhaps he just lost interest. Perhaps, with this new and captive audience, he felt like putting on a show. Perhaps he had had a hard day and wanted to relax. Whatever the motivation, he started talking about what was going on in his presidential life. For two extravagant hours he gave us a highly personal tour. He was vivid, vitriolic, scatological and extremely funny. Occasionally one of us would ask a question about something he said, but it was really a sustained monologue. He never indicated that a single word of it was "off the record" or "you can't repeat this." He was too big, too monstrous for that kind of nonsense.

I don't recall his saying anything about his fatal burden, the Vietnam War, or about his magnificent achievements, his Great Society and his civil rights laws. It was all politics and personalities. This was the old Master of the Senate who knew where every body was buried.

Although he did not personally attack his predecessor, John Kennedy, who had made him vice president, he frequently laid into "those Kennedys." He plainly despised and hated and feared Bobby Kennedy, repeatedly holding him up to sharp ridicule. He mocked his own popular Vice President Hubert Humphrey, always referring to him as "Hu-u-u-bert," as though the name alone was ludicrous (as perhaps it is).

The forever FBI Director J. Edgar Hoover, long the most feared man in Washington, was lightly tossed off as an old fairy (I later wondered what the silent Walter Jenkins thought about that) but "very useful" to a president. Hoover sent Johnson all the super-secret FBI reports about everything and everybody, and Johnson said he read them with great relish. "Best reading in town!" He described how one evening right here in the White House, he was idly watching a television attack by a leading opposition senator, while at the same time reading a juicy FBI report about who was patronizing an elegant new Washington whorehouse. "Here is this son of a bitch attacking my morals on TV, and here he is right here in the report fucking a hundred dollar whore!" A whoop of laughter, a slam-grasp of emphasis on Dick Stolley's right thigh, another bruise.

I have no idea how long this might have gone on, but at eleven o'clock Lady Bird Johnson walked into the room wearing a bright red, floor-length kimono. Bedtime everybody. It was plain that she was here to prevent her husband from staying up talking all night. She told him it was getting very late.

After acknowledging her, Johnson asked if any of us would like anything to eat. Of course we said no, it was plainly time to leave.

Johnson asked, "Bird, is there any of that tapioca left from dinner?"

Reluctantly she admitted there was, and he asked for a bowl. She brought one in and he gobbled it up.

Now at last we would leave. He walked us all down the corridor, our LIFE crew and Fortas and Jenkins, taking his time, still talking, turning off an occasional light switch, just as we all knew he did every night to save White House electric bills. He stopped at a lighted door.

"Well," he said, "this is where I get my massage every night. Helps me to sleep."

He waved a general goodbye, walked in and closed the door behind him.

We did publish the two articles and they did make a fuss. And of course Johnson did not deny anything.

A GENIAL NIGHT AT THE WHITE HOUSE

On July 19, 1978, some fourteen years after my monstrous night with LBJ, I spent another private evening in the White House with President Jimmy Carter and his wife, Rosalynn. This one lasted four hours, and the atmosphere could hardly have been more different. The aftermath, one week later in the pages of *Time*, could hardly have been worse. Thirty years later I am still embarrassed.

A year-and-a-half into his presidency Carter was getting heavy criticism from the press. The White House decided to give a series of informal, off-the-record dinners with small press groups, "a chance to get to know each other better." The first invited group came from *Time*. There were a lot of us, but the main players were the two corporate editors, Henry Grunwald and I, *Time*'s M.E. Ray Cave and its Washington Bureau Chief Robert Ajemian. A significant bonus was that Grunwald and I were invited to bring our wives, Beverly and Eleanor, and Ajemian to bring his wife, Betty. The behind-the-scene benefit of our wives' presence was an extra reward.

Thanks to an accident I have a complete record of that night.

I was never a paper squirrel. Many of my colleagues saved every scrap of paper that crossed their desks — for their files, for reference, for proof of their own innocence or somebody else's guilt, for historical record, for sheer pride. I always thought that except for a contract or a memorable memo, every piece of paper, once dealt with, should be thrown in the wastebasket. When I retired from Time Inc. after thirty-five years of paper clutter, I was asked to send all my records to Archives. I did. Next day I got a slightly hysterical phone call from the head of Archives: "Where's all the rest of it?"

But on the occasion of the Carter White House dinner, my good friend Bob Ajemian, a paper squirrel, had saved my five-page, single-spaced report and has sent it to me. So here, condensed but hot off the press three decades ago, is that evening.

When our cars arrived at the ground entrance to the White House, the President was waiting at the door to greet us. He shook hands with each of us, and a White House photographer took pictures of each couple with the president. We had cocktails in the long hall in the second floor family quarters. A number of chairs had to be dragged over to accommodate us all, and the President dragged his share. Cocktails were white wine and fruit juice passed around on trays by the all-black staff. Both Carters had wine. (Ajemian learned the next day that Rosalynn had expected to serve real cocktails to the hard-drinking press and was disappointed when they were not.)

Dinner in the long family dining room, the same room and maybe the same table as the night with LBJ, but this time there were fourteen of us. Half lobsters, small filet-size steaks with mushroom caps, zucchini casserole, croissants, a very gaudy peach melba, red and white wines and coffee. Conversation was relaxed and easy, not always general.

After dinner Rosalynn asked the wives if anybody would like to use the ladies' room before she took them on a tour. My wife Eleanor said please, pursuing her life-long belief that whenever you are offered a chance to see something different, say yes.

Rosalynn took her to the Carters' own bathroom where, with surprising informality, Rosalynn's underwear was hanging up to dry behind the shower curtain, and her nightgown hung on the bathroom door. During the subsequent tour of all the family quarters on both the second and third floors she stayed informal, volunteering information before our wives could ask questions.

The President took the men back to the cocktail area for what struck all of us as a remarkably candid conversation. If he held back on any answers, as I'm sure he did, it was not apparent. His remarks were off the record but so long ago that I don't think he would mind my mentioning a few snippets.

• On Middle East negotiations he found Egypt's Sadat "flexible" but Israel's Begin "a real obstacle to peace."

• Brezhnev was no longer physically able to negotiate, but the Russians would prepare their answers off-stage, then bring Brezhnev back to the table next day to deliver them. He and Brezhnev occasionally exchanged long letters, and Carter had tried the hot line "just to make sure it works."

• As a Washington outsider he had been amazed at how powerful and superbly organized the lobbying interests were. He had just lost two important bills to these special interests.

• He was surprisingly good-humored about most of the heat he had been taking.

• Camp David meant a lot to them, they go every weekend they can. They wear blue jeans, and Rosalynn wears no makeup.

• Despite all his Administration's difficulties he loves the job. "I can't wait to get up every morning."

We had been told to have our cars pick us up at 9:30, but the President seemed in no hurry to get rid of us. In fact, at 10:15 Grunwald and Cave apologized about having to catch the last plane back to New York. We all said goodbye to the Carters, and the Grunwalds and Cave rushed off in the first elevator.

As the rest of us were about to go down on the second trip, Carter, at Rosalynn's suggestion, asked "Have you got just another minute? I want to show you the Truman Balcony." We all followed him to the balcony — full moon, beautiful night — and he explained that he and Rosalynn loved the spot, often had breakfast there, read the newspapers. He pointed out several big rocking chairs that he said were made in Marietta, Georgia, and were the world's most comfortable.

After ten minutes on the balcony we returned to the elevator and said goodbye again. But the President rode down with us and stood in the driveway before a third and final goodbye.

What more could the Carters possibly have done to improve this special evening? They were perfect hosts — gracious, friendly, relaxed, forthcoming, generous. I was deeply impressed.

So I was deeply shocked to learn that *Time*'s planned

lead story the following week was a scathing attack on Carter's performance as President. This critique had been in the works and now was all set to run. I read the draft. Even allowing for the Administration's difficulties, it was unduly harsh. In the light of the evening we had just spent at the White House, I thought it must not be published, certainly not this coming week. Since it was not a breaking news story but only an opinion piece, simple courtesy demanded that it be postponed.

I immediately tackled Editor-in-Chief Hedley Donovan. He already knew all about our White House evening. I strongly objected to the proposed story. I said that it would be morally and socially improper to publish, and that it could only be read as a deliberate, calculated slap at the President. Hedley heard me out. Then Mr. Integrity said the story, like all stories, had to stand on its own merits. We could not allow ourselves to be influenced by extraneous factors.

I thought that was all wrong, but it was a waste of time to argue when he had decided. "Then at least postpone it."

He shook his head. "That would not be right."

When the *Time* story appeared, word came from Washington that President Carter guessed it hadn't been such a good idea to invite the press to the White House.

MR. INTEGRITY, MR. INTRANSIGENT

Hedley Donovan, who succeeded Henry Luce as editor-in-chief but not as Proprietor, was imposing. Six feet three, strongly handsome, physically and facially, with iron gray hair. He was a powerful visual presence as Luce had never been. He was a surprise choice because he was the managing editor of the relatively small magazine *Fortune* instead of one of the giants, *Time* or LIFE.

During World War II he had been a lieutenant commander in the navy, and he never got over it. Nothing rare about that. George Hunt, my managing editor at LIFE for eight years, never got over being a decorated combat officer in the Marines. But the residue of Hunt's experience was a gung ho enthusiasm, a conviction that we could take any hill, win any battle. He was great fun to work for. Hedley Donovan's residue was a chill, by-the-book formality, a severity of speech and attitude, even posture. He was no fun to work for — but you could always trust him. He was widely praised for his integrity, which was saluted by several speakers during his retirement ceremony.

He was a cinch to admire and respect. He was not easy to like.

I spent several years reporting directly to Donovan, first for a year as his sole deputy on the corporate thirty-fourth floor, then for four years as the last managing ed-

itor of LIFE, and then again on the thirty-fourth floor as
corporate editor, contending with one other editor to become Hedley's successor as editor-in-chief.

During my entire time on thirty-four, I sat in the office
immediately adjacent to Hedley's huge corner lair. Although we often consulted a dozen times a day, he virtually never appeared in my office. Instead, his secretary
walked in to tell me, "Mr. Donovan would like to see
you." In person she always addressed him as "Hedley"
(everybody on a first-name basis), but her summons was
from "Mr. Donovan." The lieutenant commander wished
to see his subordinate. He took his job, his position, his
personal responsibility and his image very seriously — but
only inside the Time-Life Building. Away from the office,
where he no longer had to be editor-in-chief, he was lively,
entertaining, witty and a three-martini drinker. His tall,
popular wife, Dorothy, encouraged all this. Going to dinner and the Metropolitan Opera with them, as my wife
and I sometimes did, made a delightful evening. Hedley
was a passionate, lifelong opera buff. He had four reserved aisle seats in row E, he had attended every opera
you ever heard of, and he had wonderful stories to tell
about individual performances and singers. He boasted
that in all his years of attendance he had never once fallen
asleep, "although once at the orchestral introduction to
the second act of *Tristan*, I may have dozed slightly."

But back in the office with Hedley was hard going,
not just for me but for all his top editors. Once he had
made up his mind — and he always made up his mind —
he would not change. You could argue, you could try to
persuade, you could even present new facts. Nothing
worked.

Like all good editors, he read advance copies of important articles before publication. During my years as LIFE's M.E., I was often called up to his office to discuss such an article. Seated at his desk, looking stonily across at me, he would say in a quiet but solemn voice, "I have a few bothers." Sounds harmless, but I soon learned that this meant many troubles, the need for many changes and inserts and fixes. Sometimes after all that work he would wind up killing the story. It didn't matter how much the story meant to me or the magazine or my staff. He was intransigent.

Hedley's most damaging obstinacy was the Vietnam War. Like the rest of the country in the late sixties, the Time Inc. staff was deeply split. But as the months and the casualties and the terrible cost went on and on, more and more of us turned against it. Not Hedley. He had made up his mind. He urged his magazines to do pro-war stories. He challenged our anti-war reporting from Vietnam and Washington. He wrote long signed editorials in LIFE insisting that we must stay the course and that we would triumph in the end.

He stuck with the war almost as long as President Johnson and the generals before he finally conceded. I had found his position embarrassing. But because he was Hedley Donovan, a man of exemplary integrity, I honored his conviction.

Besides, in his memoir he credited me as one of his three editors who had finally made him change his mind.

SOUR GRAPES

My wife Eleanor who worked at Time Inc. as long as I did, and who knew even more about office politics than I did, told me I should not write this chapter about Henry Grunwald. "It can only sound," she said, "like sour grapes."

Valid point. When Hedley Donovan took mandatory retirement in 1979, he had to pick his successor as editor-in-chief. There were only two serious candidates, and he chose Grunwald over me. I did not find this a wise or welcome decision, although it was certainly defensible.

Henry Anatole Grunwald was a brilliant, legendary writer and editor at Time Inc. He was born in Vienna, the son of a successful operetta librettist. When his Jewish family fled Austria, he came to America at age eighteen, graduated from NYU, became a *Time* copy boy and hurtled up through every rank to become *Time*'s youngest managing editor.

As a high-ranking LIFE editor I was invited to his inaugural dinner. Most acceptance speeches on these occasions are humble, grateful and sanctimonious, but Grunwald chose to quote an obscure medieval pope: "Since God has given us the papacy, let us enjoy it."

He was intellectual, well read — especially in the arts,

history and world affairs — and well informed about everything except American sports, where his ignorance and lack of interest were monumental. One of the challenges to his various administrations was to keep him separated from the *Time* sports department and, later, from our magazine *Sports Illustrated*. Fortunately, all parties were eager to cooperate in this avoidance, including Henry himself.

He was two years older than I, perhaps five feet eight, with short, crinkly gray hair and thick horn-rimmed glasses. He had a stocky, pear-shaped body, an avocado shape. In fact, because of his great success with women staff members, he was nicknamed, in envy as well as jest, the Horny Avocado. He strikingly resembled his friend Henry Kissinger. Once when an elevator door opened to reveal Grunwald and Kissinger descending from lunch in a corporate dining room, an editor said, "Ah, Tweedledum and Tweedledee!"

Henry had a fetish of meeting, collecting and first-naming national and world leaders. He knew everybody, and everybody knew him. He was indeed a world citizen.

I offer a brief summary of my competing credentials for the role of editor-in-chief. I could not compare with Henry in his many excellences. I was much more an inside-the-company than an outside man. I was a better manager and I was better at handling people. Perhaps most important, I could make up my mind and then act.

I have said that once Hedley Donovan made up his mind, he would not change it. Henry Grunwald could not make up his mind. This is not my insight. During his years as *Time* M.E. Henry was famous for his last-minute indecisions on the magazine's frantic closing night. While all the editors, writers, researchers and art directors were trying to put the magazine to bed, Henry dithered: changes in the cover, the cover billing, the lead story. He would call back a story he had already approved with his "HAG" initials and dictate a few final changes.

In salute to this disruptive behavior somebody needle-pointed a small sampler that read, "The Editor's Indecision Is Final." Henry, who had the charm of self-deprecation, hung it on his office wall for all to laugh at.

When he became editor-in-chief, I was named editorial director, a fairly rare title at Time Inc. I also joined Henry on the company's board of directors. I remained his deputy for five years. We both had summer homes on Martha's Vineyard, so we were together not only at the office but sometimes even during vacations. He was excellent company, always lively in conversation. Without ever being close friends, we got along well. But he never did learn to make up his mind.

For the best example, we explored, developed and designed a brand new magazine that Henry thought up all by himself. It was to be a monthly called *Quality*. I thought then and think now that it was a splendid idea. It could have become a small but elite success, a distinguished credit to the company that had recently launched *People*, the most spectacular instant success in magazine history but hardly an elite contribution to our image. *Quality* would supply a nice balance and contrast.

Henry's magazine had a simple, easily defined theme, always highly desirable for any new publishing venture. In gorgeous color pictures and luxurious text printed on the glossiest paper, it would celebrate quality in every field of life. Readers who cherished quality in their own lives or who longed to attain it would pay the lofty subscription price. This was obviously a home delivery magazine, not a newsstand grab like *People*.

We (chiefly Henry) proceeded to think up story ideas, shoot pictures, assign articles, make layouts, create dummies. The publishing side did analyses of potential circulation, pricing, advertising potential, expectation of losses before reaching breakeven. In the world of top magazines that Time Inc. led, launching a new magazine was big, heady stuff. *Launch* was the appropriate term we all used: an expensive aircraft carrier sliding down the ways into the open ocean.

For two years Henry fiddled through a reeling succession of art directors and layouts and story ideas and changing concepts and new departments and cover designs and typefaces. He even monkeyed with changing the title from *Quality* to *Q*. Everything he tried looked good (almost) but not quite good enough (we can do better), so let's try this or that. He kept on trying this or that, unable or unwilling to bang down the lid.

But in his slow search for *Quality*'s perfection, Henry lost momentum with the new business leaders of Time Inc. They had taken over the publishing side at the same time that Henry and I had taken over edit. Unlike them, Henry Grunwald had arrived at his new peak with a towering reputation and a long record of achievement. They were in awe of him. In that first year or so he could have done almost anything he wanted. If he had said, with all his eloquence and vigor, "Let's go with *Quality*," I bet we would have launched. But as months passed and as they got used to him, the awe dissipated. He became another thirty-fourth floor figure like themselves, a familiar colleague with recognizable shortcomings just like everybody else. I don't know if he realized this was happening. We never talked about it.

After all the start-up expense and effort that had gone into *Quality*, we never even put out a test issue. Thanks in very large part to Henry's prolonged indecision, we never published at all. In the end *Quality* didn't launch, it sank.

During Henry's eight-year tenure, two other new magazines came under serious exploration, and one was actually published. Neither was his idea, and he started with a low opinion of both. On both he preserved his native indecision.

Picture Week was to be a cheapo version of *People,* another weekly with all black-and-white pictures. But unlike all our other magazines, we would not expensively assign our own photographers. Instead, we would pick up pictures for a pittance from newspapers, wire services, picture agencies, amateur submissions. Brief headlines, brief text and captions. This project, which Henry at first deplored, then reconsidered, then eventually supported, went through actual test issues on the newsstands before it was abandoned for financial reasons.

The third magazine was Time Inc.'s grandest fiasco, *TV-Cable Week.* Christopher Byron, a Time Inc. writer, tells the full story in his savage book, *The Fanciest Dive.* The title refers to a poem about a man who makes a superb dive into an empty pool.

TV-Cable Week was a business-side notion. The theory, based on the proliferation of cable television systems in the late '70s and early '80s, was that both the system owners and the system subscribers would welcome a weekly guide to all the channels playing in their area. Providing such information in separate magazines, system by system, required an extravagant computer set-up. Surrounding the guide pages would be lively edit news and features. The total package would be thirty-two pages every week, with a different edition for each system that signed up.

Henry and I talked about it. Neither of us could drum up much excitement for a magazine of TV listings and TV news, but of course it was our responsibility, along with all the edit staff, to make it as good as possible. Henry refused to take any stand. He said that because of business-side enthusiasm, the magazine was going to happen anyway, so what was the point of arguing. I disagreed. I had studied the detailed business plan and thought it far too optimistic. The assumptions were largely untested hearsay.

I finally wrote a confidential memo to three people: to the President Richard Munro, to the head of the Magazine Group Kelso Sutton and to Henry Grunwald himself. Despite its confidentiality it soon got around and quickly became known as the Russian Roulette memo.

I said the plan was counting on too many good things happening one after another. We were counting on the cable system owners buying our magazine, which they had never seen. We were counting on a number of them buying quickly. Then we were counting on their cable subscribers buying our magazine, which they had never seen, and at a higher level of acceptance than we had ever achieved with any of our magazines. And then we were counting on a higher renewal rate than ever. I added several other dire warnings. I concluded that this was like playing Russian Roulette, where we had to keep on pulling the trigger, and every chamber had to come up empty.

Munro and Sutton did not respond. Henry told me that it was a good memo, but he doubted that it would change anything. It didn't.

So we launched *TV-Cable Week*. All their assumptions were indeed wrong. There was a bullet in every chamber. It lasted less than six months and lost $47 million.

When my thirty-fifth anniversary came around in 1983, I decided it was time to take early retirement. I was only fifty-eight, but much as I had loved all those years, enough was enough. I had nowhere further to go, and I wanted to do other things. Henry Grunwald, in a creative burst remarkable even for him, gave me three farewell parties.

He made the board of directors host a splendid dinner, where they presented me with a beautiful landscape painting of Martha's Vineyard by an artist Henry and I both admired. Then Henry put on a gala auditorium evening attended by the top edit staff of all our magazines, well over two hundred people. The entertainment for this event was a live orchestra playing an obscure piece of classical music, followed by a play in which Henry had somehow dragooned two famous figures into service.

Norman Mailer, in a gaudy uniform jacket, represented me and sang, in parody of Gilbert & Sullivan, "I am the very model of a modern major editor." Super-model Christie Brinkley, in an unforgettably short skirt, portrayed photographer Margaret Bourke-White. A bit weak on content perhaps but high on star power and audience delight.

The third party was a formal dinner at the great French restaurant La Cote Basque for 101 of my closest friends and colleagues. I can be precise about that number because Henry persuaded the Cote Basque chef to create for dessert 101 individual Grand Marnier soufflés — and to serve them simultaneously.

At each of the three parties speeches abounded. At each party Henry's was the best.

Henry might have remained editor-in-chief until his own retirement, but in 1987 President Ronald Reagan, prodded first by Mike Wallace and then by Reagan's wife, Nancy, appointed him ambassador to Austria. For a Jewish boy who had been forced to flee his country, this was a signal and appropriate honor. Henry, being Henry, saw no reason why he shouldn't keep both honors. Take a leave of absence from Time Inc., serve two years in Vienna, then return in triumph as editor-in-chief. But he was persuaded that he could not possibly be both a U.S. Government official and an independent journalist.

I think the finest achievement of Henry's great career came after his retirement.

Of course he wrote a book, we all did that. *One Man's America* was his autobiography, enriched by extensive analysis of his adopted country's values and short-comings. Well done, well reviewed.

Then came a terrible blow for a man to whom reading and writing were a major part of his life. He contracted macular degeneration. This was way before the recent advances in treatment and helpful devices. He quickly lost vision and soon could neither read nor write.

For most people this would have been crippling. Instead, Henry chose to research his own disease and to write about it, first as an article in the *New Yorker*, then in an expanded short book called *Twilight: Losing Sight, Gaining Insight*. Since he couldn't read, he hired a researcher and gave her instructions about where to find what he wanted to know. She went off to the library, to medical journals, to interviews. When she reported back, she had to read the information aloud to him. He listened, memorized, thought of additional questions and sent her back for more details. When at last he had all he needed, he dictated his story. His manuscript was read back to him, and he made editing changes as he listened.

I do not consider this humanly possible.

And Henry was not through. He decided to write a novel. Actually a modern stream-of-consciousness novel might not have been too impossible to tackle, given his eyesight, but he made it as difficult as possible. At some point in his voluminous reading he had once come across a medieval French woman who might or might not have been a saint, a subject of considerable dispute centuries ago. She had stuck in his mind, and now he would write an historical novel about her.

Back to his researcher, back to the library, back to

verbal reports and, eventually, back to a dictated manuscript. And indeed his novel was finished and published as *A Saint, More or Less*.

I wonder if by choosing this supremely arcane subject, Henry was just showing off. Probably. He was, after all, a lifelong showman. But always first class.

THE BEST MAN

For a good reason I have not written about Andrew Heiskell. He and I wrote his memoir together, a full-length book called *Outsider, Insider*. We had fun doing it, and we told everything we thought was lively, interesting and important.

But there was one thing he could not say in the book, so I will say it for him here. He was the best man in Time Inc. Not the most important — that had to be Henry Luce — but the best. He joined LIFE as a very young science and medicine editor who knew nothing about either science or medicine, but managed to fool everybody.

After two years as a writer-editor he switched over to the business side. He was the very young publisher of LIFE during its best years, and he was chairman of Time Inc. for its twenty best years. Along the way he started the hugely successful Time-Life Books Division and the even more successful *People* Magazine. Outside the building he was chairman of the New York Public Library and a leading philanthropist and fund-raiser for many worthy causes.

He was six feet four and strikingly handsome. He married both the famous movie star Madeleine Carroll and Marian Sulzberger, whose family owns the *New York Times*. Everybody admired Andrew, everybody liked him.

He was our best.

VILLAIN OF THE YEAR

Ever since 1927 *Time* has chosen a Man of the Year, later amended to Person of the Year. This was a great editorial stunt. Readers indulged in preliminary speculation and sent in their nominations. The announcement was always good for publicity in newspapers, TV and radio. Sometimes the choice was obvious (a newly elected president), sometimes perverse (the Duke and Duchess of Windsor), sometimes absurd (you, the reader). Sometimes unpopular (Adolf Hitler), sometimes wildly popular (Charles Lindbergh, the first MOY).

Each year *Time*'s choice was a closely held secret in order to protect the impact of the announcement. Even top editors on Time Inc.'s other magazines, including me at LIFE, never knew in advance. In fact, many editorial staff members of *Time* didn't know either, and those who had to know — a few key editors, writers, researchers — were sworn to secrecy.

When I became editorial director of the company in 1979, I not only got inside the secret tent but became one of the final three deciding voters. The others were Editor-in-Chief Henry Grunwald and *Time* Managing Editor Ray Cave. It was a bizarre and frustrating experience.

That word "voter" is slightly misleading. Grunwald had the final authority, and if he had wanted a Man of the Year that Cave and I didn't want, his choice would have prevailed. However, Henry Grunwald was a collegiate boss, always eager to listen to and participate in argument, constitutionally unwilling to make up his mind until it was absolutely unavoidable.

Time had some editorial traditions that we at LIFE did not share. For example, don't put anybody on the cover who has just died. Instead, always look ahead. This reached its peak of absurdity when Kennedy didn't make *Time*'s cover the week he was assassinated. Lyndon Johnson, the new president, made it instead. Another *Time* tradition was that the Man of the Year should be the person who had had the greatest impact on that year's news — for better or worse, for good or evil. Although Man of the Year was thought by *Time*'s readers and the media and the general public to be the magazine's greatest accolade, *Time* reserved the right to pick some frightful villain.

And so we come to 1979. As a member of the final triumvirate, I saw all the nominations that had come from outside and inside the magazine, along with the best arguments made by the best editors and writers. When the final, decisive meeting took place behind closed doors in Henry Grunwald's office, the choice had narrowed to two candidates.

Ayatollah Khomeini, the revolutionary clerical leader of Iran, had seized fifty-two American hostages from our embassy in Teheran. This was in retaliation for the U.S. granting asylum to the deposed shah of Iran. So far, all negotiations to make Khomeini release the hostages had failed. Americans were furious, outraged by this insult to our citizens and to our country.

Pope John Paul II had not been in office very long, and his powerful worldwide impact would not be felt for some years. But he was the first Polish pope ever, and he now held the highest office in Christendom.

I thought John Paul should be MOY. Henry Grunwald and Ray Cave agreed that he was a worthy and significant figure, but they thought that Khomeini had had the greatest impact, for good or evil, on the year's news. I couldn't disagree with that analysis, but I argued that Khomeini would be an extremely unpopular choice. I was overruled.

Henry Luce had once said to me in a private conversation, "I always thought it was the business of *Time* to make enemies, and the business of LIFE to make friends."

He was not criticizing either of his two most successful magazines but only characterizing them — brilliantly, I thought.

Luce would have been vindicated by the selection of Khomeini as MOY. It made many thousands of enemies for *Time*. Indignation and vituperation were instantaneous and universal. Those were responses that *Time*, in its editorial arrogance, could live with. What it could not live with, especially on the business side, were many, many thousands of subscription cancellations and furious threats from major advertisers to desert the ship, right now and possibly forever.

A desperate, full-scale public relations recovery act must take place at once. A very high-level editor must make a countrywide tour of TV and radio stations to explain why we had chosen Khomeini. The pitch would go like this:

We weren't saluting Khomeini. On the contrary, we

hate Khomeini as much as you do. Maybe even more. But we once chose Hitler, and we once chose Stalin, because our guiding criterion has always been who had the greatest impact on the year's news, for better or for worse. This year we deliberately chose for worse. Don't blame us, blame that monster Khomeini.

Okay, who will make this high-level p.r. trip? Henry Grunwald refused, he was too busy running all our magazines. I also think he felt it would be demeaning. Ray Cave was thought to be too combative, not genial enough to soothe the troubled waters. If some interviewer asked him a provocative question, he might well lose his temper.

So, guess who?

I survived the trip without losing my temper and without ever saying that I had been personally opposed to the selection of Khomeini. I'm not sure how much good my tour did, but at least we got an extended hearing all over the country.

More important, *Time* learned its lesson. In 2001, after the destruction of the World Trade Towers, it was perfectly, totally, inescapably obvious that the person who had had the greatest impact on that year's news, for better or worse, was Osama Ben Laden. Yes, but let's not do that again!

Time's Man of the Year in 2001 was New York City Mayor Rudi Giuliani.

THE END

LIFE closed down as a weekly magazine on December 8, 1972. The reasons are given in a speech I made three months later to the Orlando Press Club in Florida, reprinted here. The only thing I would add today is that LIFE made a gigantic effort, all through the 1950s and 1960s, to compete with television in the sheer number of our readers versus TV's sheer number of viewers. We gave the magazine away to our subscribers, far below cost, trying to beat TV's ever-growing numbers, and we tried to make our advertisers pay the difference. It is easy to see now that this was a battle we could not win.

I have often wondered what might have happened if, instead of trying to buy readers at phony prices, we had charged a proper rate and reduced our circulation to those people who really wanted the magazine and were willing to pay for it.

But that probably wouldn't have worked either.

THE DEATH OF LIFE

I think you are all very brave to be here tonight, considering that the very melancholy title of this speech was announced in advance. An awards dinner should be a cheerful affair full of congratulations and well-earned self-esteem. At such a time I do not want to be solely responsible for casting a pall. Although I think that the end of LIFE magazine was a serious and important event, I promise not to talk about it in funereal terms.

It has been less than three months since LIFE's last issue appeared, and I find that I miss it very much. Perhaps the many other journalists in this room will be as surprised as I am by the fact that I miss it more as a reader than I do as an editor. That may be because I was a LIFE editor for only eighteen years, hardly long enough to get used to it, but I've been a LIFE reader twice that long. Every since it began. As you all know, with the earlier disappearances of *The Saturday Evening Post* and *Look*, there is simply no magazine now in existence that does what LIFE tried to do.

But in spite of LIFE's end, I feel very good about a number of things, which are worth remembering in a bad time:

•LIFE was once the most successful magazine the country has ever known.

•It had more impact on its readers than any magazine in American history.

•It more than fulfilled Henry Luce's famous prepublication boast that the magazine would enable its readers "to see life, to see the world, to eyewitness great events."

•During its very difficult last years, we who worked at LIFE were given every conceivable opportunity to turn it around. LIFE was not killed coldly or casually, as it might have been at another company. Time Inc. put a great deal of money and effort and emotion into trying to save it. Only when the projections of losses for the next three years became staggering was the decision finally and reluctantly taken to drop it.

•And although we did have to stop publication, anyone who worked there at any time during the last thirty-six years had a marvelous and unforgettable experience. This was true even during the last two or three years. In fact, when the announcement was made, a young woman who had been employed for less than a month was in tears because, she said, she had already learned that this was *the* place she wanted to spend her career.

•Usually when a magazine or newspaper suspends publication, it is a disaster for the staff members, all of whom abruptly lose their jobs. This did not happen at LIFE. The reputation of the staff was such that we immediately got more than four hundred job offers from all over the country. In less than three months, all but twenty-five of the one hundred sixty edit staff members were able to find other jobs or had chosen to freelance. And those who didn't yet have jobs were getting the benefit of the largest notice and severance pay that anyone in our profession had every heard of.

As a result of all these things, the LIFE staff, including myself, emerged with their pride and dignity intact and with far less feeling of failure than one might expect. Soon after the announcement, one of our young women reporters was being interviewed for a job by an editor of one of the other Time Inc. magazines. The editor was, I'm sorry to say, rather patronizing. "Of course," the editor said, "we know that all you people on LIFE had a lot of fun, but I'm not sure you're used to the kind of hard work we do here." Our reporter was indignant. "Oh, you're *wrong*," she said. "At LIFE we worked just as hard as you do. And if you don't have any fun, that's your problem." Our reporter did not get that particular job, but the whole LIFE staff was proud of her.

LIFE had originally planned to have a Christmas party. After the announcement that seemed a little silly, but the staff voted to get together anyway for a final, farewell drink in the copy room. At that time practically everyone in that room was out of a job. An extraordinary picture was taken at that party. Some 125 faces are clearly identifiable, and almost every one of them is cheerful, smiling. It is a picture of a large group of friends who plainly enjoy each other's company, even though it is for the last time.

The event of LIFE's folding was indeed a shock to us but not, after all, a surprise. I know that all of you have been reading about LIFE's troubles for a long time. God knows I have. All through the last three and a half years while I was managing editor, I got many, many phone calls from reporters, asking me if the rumor was true that LIFE was folding. I was always able to answer truthfully that the rumor was *not* correct, but this didn't stop the phone calls. Three of these reporters became absolute regulars: the *New York Times*, *Newsweek* and *Women's Wear Daily*. Sometimes only one of them would call me, but if it was a really lively rumor period, I could count on hearing from all three. I was rather testy and vigorous the first few times around the rumor track, but after a while my regulars and I got quite friendly and relaxed about it. We got on a first-name basis, and eventually we were all making little jokes and apologies about having to go through the routine again. Sometimes I would chide one of them for being late to call. I had so many talks with my regulars and with other reporters that everybody got tired of it. In the final two weeks before the announcement I didn't get a single call about any rumor that LIFE was folding. It may have been the only two-week period in my entire stint as managing editor when I didn't get such a call. That was most fortunate. It spared me from having to lie or obfuscate, and besides, there were many other things to think about during that time.

Everyone in LIFE management on both the publishing and editing sides was familiar with our strenuous problems. We had gone through enormous budget and staff and circulation cuts, all very painful. We had several times been through the lengthy exercise of studying radical change, perhaps switching to a biweekly, perhaps reducing page size to save on LIFE's huge paper and mailing costs. At one point in 1971 we actually did decide to change LIFE to a biweekly, but then later projections came in on the damage this would do to advertising pages, and the decision was reversed.

So we had all been living in a precarious economy for

many months when, on the morning of last November 27, Editor-in-Chief Hedley Donovan called to ask if I could have lunch with him. As you know, the answer to this question from the editor-in-chief is, "Yes, of course." But on this occasion I said that I had invited a TIME correspondent named Bonnie Angelo to come up from Washington, have lunch with three LIFE editors and become LIFE's new Washington bureau chief. I explained that it would be awkward to get out of it since she had already left Washington. There was a long pause to which, at the time, I attached no significance. Then Mr. Donovan asked if I could have dinner with him instead, since he needed a couple of hours of uninterrupted talk.

That night in a private dining room with the door closed so that waiters could not overhear, I learned that all the projections for LIFE's cost and losses for the next few years looked hopelessly large — even if we went to a biweekly, even if we reduced circulation. All the figures were being worked over, and an effort was still being made to find some palatable formula for keeping LIFE alive, but if the figures didn't change, the outlook was grim. I was asked to say nothing to anyone, because the situation might still change, and because the board of directors had made no decision.

I had lived with the LIFE crisis for so long that I literally did not realize until the following morning, when I had a second talk with the editor-in-chief, that this time the patient's condition was terminal.

The most difficult thing about the next ten days was that LIFE magazine went on as usual. We closed a special issue about Christmas, we did advance work on another special issue, the Year in Pictures, with no one realizing that it might be the last issue of LIFE. Staff members held meetings to plan their story assignments for the first part of 1973. An opening had turned up in our Paris bureau, and one of the assistant managing editors kept bringing me promising candidates for a job that we would never be able to fill. One of our Paris correspondents had already been named to take over the Hong Kong bureau, and he was busily packing up his family and household belongings to ship them to the Far East. I found out that he was not planning to leave right away. I don't know what I would have done had he said he was leaving a week earlier. Bonnie Angelo, the TIME correspondent we had asked to be our new Washington bureau chief, accepted with enthusiasm and naturally wanted to know when it would be announced. I stalled. Meantime there was no change in the projected numbers. And still no phone calls from reporters.

On Tuesday, December 5, the board of directors, after hearing all the gloomy evidence, gave its executive committee the authority to set a special meeting late Thursday afternoon, if no new evidence was forthcoming that might change LIFE's prospects.

If you have not recently been involved in the folding of a major property, you probably have no idea what complexities are provided by the Securities and Exchange Commission and the National Labor Relations Board. The SEC requires that when a company makes a decision that might have an important effect on the stock, the stock exchange must be notified at the earliest opportunity. And the NLRB regulations require that if a company makes a decision that will have an important effect on employees' jobs, the Newspaper Guild must be notified as soon as possible.

On Thursday evening, December 7, after the country's stock exchanges had closed for the day, the executive committee met in the Time-Life Building and made the decision to close LIFE. The same evening Hedley Donovan invited the ten top LIFE editors to his office and told them of the decision. For them it was the first time they had heard the news. Then we trooped down to my office, closed the doors and — as journalists tend to do on momentous occasions — had a drink together.

I was deeply concerned that the LIFE staff members should learn the bad news directly from the company, and not from the AP or UPI ticker or a phone call from some outsider. Mr. Donovan and Chairman of the Board Andrew Heiskell had already planned a 10:30 meeting of the entire staff for the following morning to tell them of the decision. But no notice of such a meeting could be sent out until and unless the executive committee decided to suspend publication. The notice was secretly mimeographed in advance, in case the worst happened. Now it would be distributed first thing in the morning. But as I told the LIFE editors having a drink in my office that Thursday night, a number of staff members might not get the notice in time. Some of them would be out on stories. Also, because of the special issue we were closing, some of them who were not involved might easily come in late or do some Christmas shopping on their way to work.

One editor suggested calling them at home that night to tell them to come in next morning for a special meeting, but we all knew what would happen. First, they would want to know what it was about, and when we couldn't tell them, they would get on the phone to each other, and finally somebody in the outside press would hear about it, and one way or another the news would be out — before the meeting and before the SEC and the Newspaper Guild had been properly notified. And yet we could not let our colleagues, many of whom had worked with us for ten or twenty years, miss the meeting.

We finally dug out a stack of home address lists, and the ten of us went through the entire staff, name by name, deciding who was going to telephone whom at home the first thing Friday morning. We would not be able to tell them what the meeting was about, but at that late hour no harm would be done if anyone guessed. Each of us wound up with a list of a dozen or more people to call. Those who lived in the suburbs would be called first, so they would have time to catch their trains, and those who lived in the city would be called just in time to get to the meeting.

As we were parceling out this task, my secretary knocked on the door and then opened it to say the Rockefeller Center police had a report that a bomb had been planted on our floor. Security officers were all over the floor and they wanted to warn us that somebody might be trying to blow up the place. We all looked at each other in sudden wild humor. Our particular world had already blown up. The photography editor was the quickest. "Tell 'em it's too late!" he said.

We closed the door and went on with our work. It gave all of us something useful to do at a time when there was really nothing left for us to do. I went home to work on what I trust will be the most painful speech of my life.

The next morning, Friday, December 8, the whole

staff assembled in a meeting barred to outsiders, and we told them about the end of their magazine.

One of our top editors was in Saigon that day working on a story. I finally reached him by phone and told him the news. Like me, he had been at LIFE for many years, and I think his first response spoke for all of us. "Well," he said, "some damn good years."

I do not have any revelations for you tonight about why LIFE had to be killed. You've heard them all, and they are all true. Television was the principal reason, of course, because television was able to do many of LIFE's best tricks — and do them live and in color and in motion. Television was also more popular with big advertisers who wanted to reach enormous numbers of people at a relatively low cost per person. But television was only one factor. LIFE also ran into soaring physical costs for paper and printing. And there was the shocking increase of 170% in postal rates. LIFE was also affected by the growth of special interest magazines, which give both readers and advertisers exactly what they want, with no danger that some surprising news or some subject of broader national interest might interfere with the reader's concentration. And I do not want to omit from this list of LIFE's troubles the possibility that we editors, especially me, may have been doing something wrong. As Hedley Donovan said in his announcement to the staff, "Publishing is not an exact science."

But after all these factors have been cited, I think it is fair to point out that in the end it was the reader who said, "No thanks, I don't want LIFE badly enough to pay for it." What a healthy magazine or newspaper needs is readers who will subscribe to it or buy it on the newsstand at a fair price and with reasonable regularity. Unfortunately, LIFE had trained its readers long, long ago to expect the magazine to be a bargain.

When LIFE first appeared in November 1936, you could buy it on the newsstands for a dime. Thirty years later, after more inflation and more physical costs than I could possibly calculate, the new LIFE subscriber could still get the magazine for about a dime. All through the fifties and early sixties, LIFE was playing — and winning — the numbers game. In the great numbers war with *Colliers*, *The Saturday Evening Post* and *Look* and, in the later years, television, we provided the circulation and the reader paid for some of it, and the advertisers paid for a lot of it. During those years we never asked the reader to pay his own way. During these last few years when we finally asked the subscriber to pay more — sixteen cents and seventeen cents an issue — it was too late and not enough. A number of times since becoming managing editor, I had maddening conversations with people who asked what my job was. When I told them, they would say with genuine enthusiasm and meaning to pay me a compliment, "Oh, we *love* LIFE. We subscribe to it every time you come out with one of those good offers that says 'Try LIFE for thirteen weeks at less than eleven cents an issue.'"

Well, we finally gave up that practice. The last LIFE subscriber policy was that nobody was going to get a better bargain than the long-term subscriber. But we never had a chance to find out how that would have worked. For all I know, it might have worked very badly. To repeat, "Publishing is not an exact science." What had made LIFE profitable in the 1950s didn't work at all in the 1970s, but the pattern had been established.

The obituaries on LIFE, most of which were friendly, said that what had vanished was an institution whose days were over. I have no argument with that position. I think that institutions whose day is over *should* vanish, instead of hanging around and getting in everybody's way. But I would take two exceptions. One factual, one that I will simply call spiritual.

Factually, LIFE is finished as a weekly, large-circulation magazine that you could buy dirt cheap. But Time Inc. is by no means finished with LIFE. We are keeping title to the name and the logo and to the LIFE Picture Collection, which has eighteen million images on file, the largest indexed treasure of pictures in the world. Out of that collection, we have already put together an extraordinary three-hundred-page picture book called *The Best of LIFE*. In my opinion it is the finest book of photographs every published, not because we did such a marvelous job of putting it together, but because it was drawn from all the pictures LIFE published in 1,864 issues over thirty-six years. There are eighteen chapters: Great Moments, Leaders, Entertainers, Athletes, Animals, Fads, Fashion and so on. Each chapter could have been made into an entire book, so rich is the material. No one has seen this book yet except the editors, but we did send a letter to our subscribers, inviting them to order a copy. On the first day we got 35,000 orders. On the second day the mail room told us it was too much trouble to count the orders so they were going to measure them — with a ruler. By the end of the first week the orders were up to

127,000, whether by count or by ruler, I don't know. Anyway, that's pretty good for a fifteen dollar book from an institution whose day is over.

The Best of LIFE book is not the only project. We may indeed publish other volumes. We are also discussing the possibility of bringing out one or more special issues of LIFE on single subjects to be sold on newsstands only. If we ever do that, and if that turns out to be a successful venture, it is not impossible that some time in the future we night even publish LIFE regularly again — perhaps four or six times a year. That is pure speculation at this point, but you can be sure that if such an event ever comes to pass, the price to the reader will be right — meaning higher. And the circulation will be natural — meaning that we won't spend buckets of money trying to persuade people to sign up. Meantime LIFE's influence on picture journalism lives on, not only in our other magazines — *Time, Fortune, SI* — but in most magazines and in most newspapers.

That is my factual exception. My spiritual exception is that I think LIFE was trying to do something important that should not be allowed to vanish with the magazine. I have spoken earlier tonight about special interest magazines. They have obvious appeal and an important place in publishing. However, by definition, they do have a tightly restricted kind of audience and restricted subject matter. That's fine as far as it goes. Most newspapers are also special interest publications, serving their own community or state and therefore having a natural tendency to concentrate overwhelmingly on local news.

LIFE always tried to do something different. We tried to talk to people across all barriers and special interests.

We weren't talking to our readers as skiers, or teenagers, or TV watchers, or single women, or suburbanites, or inhabitants of some particular community. We were trying to talk to our readers as people, who share the common experience of humanity. LIFE tried to be a bridge of understanding between people who need to know more about each other. For as long as we lasted, I hope we did not fail in that purpose.

LIFE can no longer serve that purpose, but I believe that the need for it still exists. If LIFE could leave one heritage to other members of the press and television, it would be to make that effort as often as you can, and as strongly as you can. For understanding one another is truly in our national interest.

CLOSING DAY

As I explained in the previous chapter, my top editors and I made a determined effort to assemble the entire staff in the auditorium for the final announcement of LIFE's demise.

It was made by Editor-in-Chief Hedley Donovan. His speech was clear, meticulous, explanatory and ice cold.

Our longtime Chairman Andrew Heiskell spoke second. He had started his career as a young LIFE science editor. He switched over to the business side and became publisher of LIFE during its most successful years, before being promoted to chairman of the whole company. He gave a short but emotional speech, tears in his eyes, about how proud we should be for all the great stories LIFE had published over the past thirty-six years.

Donovan and Heiskell had planned to be the only speakers, but before the meeting began, I told them I wanted to speak too. They were surprised, but said all right.

Three names in my brief talk need identification. Garry Valk was our last publisher. Ed Thompson was a popular and successful managing editor during the magazine's best years. Mary Leatherbee, our entertainment editor for many years, had recently drowned in a canoe accident. I thought, as did many others, that she was the quintessential LIFE editor, full of enthusiasm and story ideas and devotion to the magazine. Just a few weeks earlier we had held a memorial for Mary in this same auditorium, informal talks filled with affectionate and amusing anecdotes.

What I said that last morning is what you read here, except for the very last line. Deeply moved, I realized, as I started the final sentence, that I simply would not be able to say the two words "so gladly" without breaking down. So I left them out. But I mean what I had written: "that gift which we so gladly gave to each other."

LAST WORDS

There is nothing I can do to soften this sad blow. I do want to say how grateful I am to you for the work and the spirit that kept LIFE going as long as possible. I am especially grateful for the past year. Under all the adversities of deep personnel cuts and tight budgets and grave worries about the health of the magazine, you continued to put out weekly issues of LIFE in which we can all take pride. That is a signal achievement, and I don't know anyone who could have done it except the fine people in this room. I just want to say thank you for that — to Garry Valk's publishing side as well as to edit.

I hope the younger, newer people on the staff will forgive me, on this occasion, if I say a few words to those staff members who, like me, have been here a very long time. Many of us have spent our whole professional lives on this magazine, and we have thoroughly enjoyed doing so. We've seen each other two hundred days a year for many years, and I for one never got tired of it. That didn't keep us from bitching about the magazine or the hours or even each other, but we always kept coming back for more. We know each other better than we know anyone outside our own families.

Ed Thompson used to say that at LIFE it was all very well to be a first-class journalist, but to really enjoy it, you needed to be a bit of a slob. He always said this about himself, and he meant that no matter how many things went wrong, no matter how many packets got lost or delayed, he never lost his affection for the staff and for the magazine. That goes for me and, I trust, for you. It is a very rare thing in the American corporate world today, and now we must end it.

This is a sad ending, but I hope none of us will remember LIFE or each other in terms of this morning. We worked on a great and famous magazine, we published many wonderful stories, and we had a remarkable experience together.

Instead of this morning, I would rather remember our last meeting, which took place here in this room a few weeks ago when we got together to talk about Mary Leatherbee. A number of outsiders who attended that meeting say it made them understand for the first time why LIFE was such a special, marvelous place to work. Perhaps it even helped us insiders understand why we like being here.

I am setting up an employment committee to try to help all of you find other jobs. That is my only assignment, and I will do the best I can with it. But I won't pretend that any place else is going to be like what we shared together at LIFE. I thank you all for that gift which we so gladly gave to each other.

TWO LAST PICTURES

On December 8, 1972, the day we announced the end of
LIFE, I would have liked to spend the rest of the day in the
halls with all my friends and colleagues, sharing that last
day of memory together. Instead I had to spend that long
day behind the desk in my own office, granting interviews
to reporters from other magazines, newspapers, radio and
TV, and talking to other reporters over the phone. The
sudden end of LIFE was that day's big news, and as the
last editor I was obviously the main source for quotes and
explanations. For many years we had been a major part of
the press. Now we owed it to them to give answers.

Blah-blah-blah, dreary work, but stay polite, be careful to say the right things.

Twice during that final day a specific LIFE picture
jumped back into my mind.

Although the people entering my office were outside
reporters, allowed in one by one by my secretary, there
was a happy exception. David Scherman was the only
man in the magazine's history who converted from being
a staff photographer to a department head editor. He had
been a mediocre, okay photographer but was a first-class
editor in charge of all our regular reviews (books, movies,
TV) but, more significantly, our Close-Ups. These were
short, lively, black-and-white people stories with quotes

under every picture that ran virtually every week. He was so good that he could easily have aspired to a higher job, but he was outspokenly cynical. All of us referred to the magazine's stock in trade as "pictures," sometimes as "photos" or "photographs," or even rarely as "pix." Scherman alone irreverently called them "snaps."

This morning he was not cynical. Only an hour after the auditorium announcement of our demise, the end of everything, the end of our magazine and all our jobs, he forced his way past my secretary to tell me his terrific idea. We would publish a LIFE-size anthology of all our best pictures over the years. The best picture book ever. We'd call it *The Best of* LIFE, it would be a huge bestseller, and because it was his idea he would be the editor.

Everything Davey had just said would come true. So did the next thing he said.

"I already know what the last page is going to be."

It took only five seconds before I answered, "So do I."

Then together we said, "The monkey in the water."

This famous black-and-white picture of a rhesus monkey sitting waist deep in water and glowering straight at the camera was shot in Puerto Rico by a woman staff photographer named Hansel Mieth. The monkey's fierce but comic expression shows that he is thoroughly pissed off at this invasion of his watery privacy. It ran as the final page of an issue way back in 1939 and had been an icon ever since. Poor Hansel Mieth. No matter how many other good pictures she shot, she could never get that monkey out of the water or off her back.

The other famous image from that last day was brought to mind when one of the newspaper reporters, over the phone, asked me a different and interesting question. Looking back, what did I think was the most moving, the most memorable picture that LIFE ever ran. That took me longer than five seconds. Many contenders. But finally I said "Buna Beach."

Also black-and-white, this was taken by war correspondent photographer George Strock in February 1943. Three American soldiers lie on a sandy New Guinea beach during the early months of MacArthur's World War II Pacific campaign. They are dressed in combat fatigues and boots, and two of them are still wearing those round steel helmets. We cannot see their faces, we can only see that they are all dead.

It is a beautiful picture, perfectly composed, the three bodies stretched out calm and graceful. The sand has partially covered the legs of the first soldier, who lies face down. In the precise center of the picture. the relaxed right hand of the middle soldier is flung straight out, dead white against the sand. Behind the bodies, still in the water, is the broken hulk of a landing craft, another remnant of the recent battle that cost three thousand American lives. Against the horizon stand tropical trees. The picture is supremely quiet, utterly peaceful. The sole motion is a tiny wavelet breaking on the beach.

Although the picture was shot in February, it did not appear in the magazine until seven months later in the September 20 issue. Wartime censorship forbade publishing pictures of American dead. President Roosevelt himself rescinded this restriction because he thought his countrymen should face up to the reality of war. Buna Beach was the first published picture to bring this home.

That was what LIFE always tried to do: bring things home.